D0624234

The Organic Lunchbox

125 Yummy, Quick, and Healthy Recipes for Kids

Marie W. Lawrence

Photos by Abigail Lawrence

Skyhorse Publishing

Copyright © 2017 by Marie Lawrence

Photos copyright © 2017 by Abigail Lawrence

All rights reserved. No part of this book may be reproduced in any manner without the express written consent of the publisher, except in the case of brief excerpts in critical reviews or articles. All inquiries should be addressed to Skyhorse Publishing, 307 West 36th Street, 11th Floor, New York, NY 10018.

Skyhorse Publishing books may be purchased in bulk at special discounts for sales promotion, corporate gifts, fund-raising, or educational purposes. Special editions can also be created to specifications. For details, contact the Special Sales Department, Skyhorse Publishing, 307 West 36th Street, 11th Floor, New York, NY 10018 or info@skyhorsepublishing.com.

Skyhorse® and Skyhorse Publishing® are registered trademarks of Skyhorse Publishing, Inc.®, a Delaware corporation.

Visit our website at www.skyhorsepublishing.com.

10 9 8 7 6 5 4 3 2 1

Library of Congress Cataloging-in-Publication Data is available on file.

Cover design by Jane Sheppard
Cover photo credit: iStockphoto.com

Print ISBN: 978-1-5107-2389-4
Ebook ISBN: 978-1-5107-2390-0

Printed in China

For Lilly Cookson and Erik Cookson
with lots of love. —Granny

Table of Contents

Introduction

Children are pretty amazing people, aren't they? And amazing people deserve amazing food; especially kids, with their growing minds and bodies.

It's unfortunate that many of the foods currently marketed to children are so high in sugar, salt, unhealthy fats, and additives. I think we can all agree that consuming such foods on a regular basis does not contribute to a healthy lifestyle, or to forming positive eating habits to carry into adulthood.

However, the healthiest food in the world isn't going to do us any good unless we also want to eat it! And while many kids love a wide range of foods, chances are they're still going to prefer foods that are fun to look at, fun to eat, and, most importantly, foods that taste delicious! Over the past four decades, I've worked with hundreds of children, ranging from kindergarten through sixth grade, through my employment in public schools, as a volunteer, and, last but not least, as a mom and grandma! As part of my classroom experience, I've run cooking clubs, implemented healthy snack programs, coordinated the planting and harvesting of school gardens, and even put on a three-course French dinner for twenty second-graders! All those experiences have contributed to my understanding of what kids enjoy eating and some fun ways to facilitate that.

The Organic Lunchbox offers you a refreshing alternative to many of the prepackaged foods out there. The recipes, running the gamut from breakfast-style entrées to snacks, hearty main dishes, soups, sandwiches, salads, and even some desserts, are prepared using organically grown grains, produce, and proteins.

But what, exactly, constitutes organic? And how do these foods compare to natural, non-GMO, or BST Free? We'll be doing a little detective work to better enable us to make informed choices.

You'll find quite a bit of variety in *The Organic Lunchbox*. Some recipes are quick and easy, using only a few ingredients. Others would make great family-oriented cooking projects on a day when you have a little more time to share with your children. The vast majority of them are also kid-tested, kid-prepared, and kid-approved.

So, come and open the lunchbox with me. New eating adventures await within!

Enjoy!
Marie

Organic . . . What Does It Mean?

There certainly are a lot of different terms floating around when it comes to our food supply. Let me try to demystify a few of them for you.

According to the United States Department of Agriculture (USDA) blog page, certified organic foods are grown in accordance with a complex set of standards set forth by the USDA.

Produce must be grown without use of synthetic fertilizers or pesticides. There are a few exceptions allowed in the treatment of certain conditions, but those products must meet with the approval of the USDA and be applied only for approved purposes. Additionally, it must be proven that the soil upon which the produce is grown has met this standard for at least three years prior to the harvesting of fruits, vegetables, or herbs labeled as organic.

Animals raised to produce organic meat or milk and poultry must:

- be fed 100 percent organic feed and forage;
- not be administered growth hormones or antibiotics; and
- be allowed to live in conditions that accommodate their natural behaviors, such as cattle being allowed to graze in open pastures.

Processed foods labeled as organic are prohibited from containing artificial colors, flavors, or preservatives. There are some limited exceptions, such as the use of baking soda in baked goods, pectin in jams or jellies, or enzymes in yogurt products.

When a processed food is labeled as containing a specific organic ingredient (such as wheat in crackers), it must contain at least 70 percent organically produced ingredients. Additionally, the remaining nonorganic ingredients must have been produced in accordance with USDA regulations and without the use of prohibited practices, such as genetic engineering. While these products are not strictly organic, they do meet a goodly part of the criteria.

A genetically modified organism, a.k.a. GMO, can be any plant, animal, or organism that has had part of its genome modified, reduced, or added to. This can be accomplished through a technique called recombinant gene therapy, in which DNA from more than one species is spliced together and then introduced into a host organism. In the production of food, it may be used to produce varieties of plants that are disease-, pesticide-, or pest-resistant, or fish that grow at an abnormally accelerated rate. There is a fair amount of controversy revolving around the concept of GMOs, with proponents seeing their use as a way to end world hunger. Many others question the effects of this technology on other species, such as the possibility of "super weeds" being an inadvertent by-product. There is also concern about biotech companies "taking over" farming, or other as yet unknown factors, including but not limited to what long-term effect consumption of these products might have on human beings.

It is important to note that organically grown foods are specifically prohibited from using GMO technology. Therefore, by definition, no food labeled as organic by the USDA can be genetically modified. However, other foods that are not organically grown may also be quite accurately labeled as non-GMO if that is the manner in which they have been produced. Look for non-GMO labeling on products or do some online research.

Hybrid seeds and plants are part of a much older technology than GMO seeds and plants. They are formed when two similar varieties, often from the same species, cross-pollinate, thereby producing a slightly different variation than either parent. Early hybridization of plants by humans was a time-consuming process that could take multiple generations to produce the end product. Modern hybridization techniques speed up the process by selectively growing and cross-pollinating parent species of the two plants the grower wishes to hybridize. The resulting seeds are referred to as F1. F1 seeds and the vegetables grown from them can be marketed as either organic or not, dependent on the methodology used to produce them. Some strong proponents of non-GMO technology also do not approve of hybrid products, most likely because you cannot use the seeds produced by a hybrid crop to plant the following year; they revert back to the parent plants, rather than growing the same product. However, I don't believe this factor makes a hybrid squash or ear of corn any more or less nutritious or palatable than those produced from traditional seed. I personally grow some vegetables from hybrid seeds in my garden every year.

Recombinant Bovine Growth Hormone, abbreviated as rBGH (also referred to as Recombinant Bovine Somatotropin, or rBST), is a genetically altered hormone that is injected into some dairy cattle, causing them to produce 10–15 percent more milk than they naturally would. Although the FDA approved the use of rBST/rBGH in 1993, and in 1994 prohibited dairies from claiming there is any difference between milk produced from rBGH/rBST-injected cows and those that are not injected with it, those decisions remain controversial. Many farmers have chosen to forego use of this substance for a variety of reasons, not the least of which are the detrimental health effects suffered by the injected cows. It is noteworthy that a number of other countries ban the use of this substance entirely. If you are concerned about the use of GMOs and/or care about the health and well-being of the animals being used to produce milk, you now have even more reasons to buy organic; rBST/rBGH-free, nonorganic milk is also widely available.

Natural foods may be labeled as such if they do not contain any artificial or synthetic substances. However, according to the Food and Drug Administration (FDA) website, this does not currently address food production methods, such as the use of pesticides. It also does not specifically address manufacturing and processing methods like irradiation, pasteurization, or thermal technologies. The FDA recently sought out public input in regards to appropriate use of the "natural" designation (the comment period closed May 10, 2016), so I suspect that at some point in the future we may be seeing a more definitive use of the word.

What About Peanuts, Tree Nuts, and Seeds?

In recent years, an increasing number of children have experienced allergic reactions to peanuts. In some instances, these reactions are life-threatening; they are definitely a reason for serious concern. In response to this, a number of schools are now banning peanuts and peanut products. Some have gone further, banning tree nuts and in some cases even seeds. Approximately 40 percent of kids with peanut allergies are also allergic to one or more tree nuts.

The allergen component in peanuts is contained in the protein. While some peanut oil has been so highly refined that the protein content is mostly nonexistent, other less-refined varieties of it may indeed carry traces of protein; enough to spark an allergic reaction in a vulnerable individual. If your child has an allergy to peanuts and/or tree nuts, your physician is the person best equipped to guide you through what may be considered safe or unsafe. If you are simply unsure what to send or not send to a peanut- or tree nut-free school, I suggest you check in with the school nurse and/or administrator for guidance.

Tree nuts cover a wide range, and in many instances if a person has proven allergic to one type of nut, they may be told to avoid all tree nuts as a preventative measure. One exception that is frequently mentioned is the coconut. Although listed as a tree nut by the FDA, coconuts are actually the "seed of a drupaceous fruit." As such, they may be safe for a person with nut allergies to eat—but, again, it is essential to discuss this with your family doctor. I have included some recipes that contain coconut oil, as it is widely available in organic form. If you have been instructed to avoid coconut oil, solid vegetable shortening can usually be substituted for it.

Be sure to read labels for "hidden" ingredients. Peanut oil is frequently used to fry potato chips and is also often found in prepared Chinese and Mexican foods. Commercially produced baked goods or ice creams may also contain peanut meal, peanut oil, traces of peanuts, or may simply have been baked or mixed in close proximity to them.

Although a small number of individuals with peanut allergies also may not be able to tolerate soybeans, many people are able to consume soy with no ill effects. Soy butter has become a widely accepted alternative to peanut butter. Even though soy beans and peanuts are both legumes by definition, there seems to be less tendency to cross-reactivity between members of the legume family (peanuts, peas, beans, soybeans) than there is with certain other interrelated food groups, such as a person with an allergy to shrimp also experiencing an allergic reaction to lobster.

One challenge when using soy products is finding those that are organic, or even non-GMO. By some estimates, 90 percent of the soybeans grown in the United States have been genetically modified; and as previously mentioned, this automatically precludes them from being considered organic. According to the website organicauthority.com, brands including Eden Foods, Wildwood, Mitoku, and Tofurky are all good sources of non-GMO, organically produced soy products.

Another consideration when purchasing any food is that you want your child to enjoy eating it. For instance, when the school where I was employed banned peanuts a few years ago, the most popular soy butter among the kids was a product called Wowbutter. While it is not listed as organic, it is non-GMO and has a very informative product website. In my personal opinion, it tastes much better than some of the other soy-based products out there.

I have included some recipes with seeds in them. In general, during my searches on the subject, the seed that popped up over and over again as the most common allergen was the sesame seed. Since they are widely used to top breads and buns, chances are if your child has a sensitivity to them you're already aware of it. I haven't used sesame in any of my recipes, except for tahini as an alternative ingredient in hummus. There are a few recipes with other types of seeds in them, such as pumpkin seeds, sunflower seeds or sun butter, ground flaxseed, and poppy seeds, as these are frequently considered acceptable alternatives to peanuts and/or tree nuts. In most instances, they can simply be omitted from the recipe in question if you don't wish to use them.

Preparing Organic Meals for Your Family

Going 100 percent organic can still pose some challenges. Variables may include the area of the country you live in, whether you are in a rural or urban setting, and the eating habits of your family.

I am fortunate to live in an area where there is strong support for sustainable, locally produced, organic products, and even in this setting I faced some challenges trying to make every recipe totally from organic ingredients. In general, organic foods are still considerably more costly than nonorganic, and this may also factor into whether your diet will consist entirely of organic foods, or if there will be some combination of organic and nonorganic involved.

I'll begin with a few tips for keeping your budget workable when buying organic.

Look for fresh, organic produce in season. Stock up when there is a plentiful supply and put some aside for later use. If you have adequate freezer

space, that can be a relatively simple way to preserve some nice fresh veggies or fruits when they are at their peak. If you're not familiar with how to successfully freeze a certain item, invest in a good home guide or do a search online.

Organic herbs and spices are now widely available, but those in individual bottles can be quite expensive. Finding a store in your area that sells organic spices and herbs in bulk can result in significant price savings.

Check out both the canned goods and freezer sections at your grocery store to determine what is available. Just like you, the producers of fruits and vegetables are going to preserve their products when they are at their freshest, and they are often more economical to purchase than their fresh counterparts.

Depending on the size of the community you live in, shop at more than one store. Health food stores and cooperatives will often offer the widest selection, but general grocery stores are increasingly meeting the needs of consumers who wish to buy organic.

The easier an organic product is to produce and store, the more readily available it will be. This is why grain products, such as cereal and flour, as well as certain vegetables and fruits, will probably be easier to find than meat. Organic eggs and dairy products have also become more readily available in recent years due to customer demand.

If you have to make a choice in which items you buy that are organically produced, factor in a few considerations. Each year the Environmental Working Group analyzes Department of Agriculture data to determine which fruits and vegetables have the highest amounts of pesticide residues and rates them accordingly. They then compile a "Dirty Dozen" list, as well as a "Clean Fifteen" list, showing those nonorganically grown fruits and vegetables with the lowest levels of pesticide contamination. According to the information page on the EWG site, the American Academy of Pediatrics recommends EWG's Shoppers Guide as a resource to pediatricians when consulting with parents about reducing pesticide exposure in their children (ewg.org/foodnews/dirty_dozen_list.php).

Look for meat and poultry that has a humanely raised designation and that has been kept antibiotic-free. In beef, also look for grass-fed and/or grass-pastured; in poultry and eggs, look for cage-free and antibiotic-free. If you have a local butcher shop, check in with them about the sources of their meat.

Sometimes knowing your source can be an important factor in deciding whether to go strictly organic or not. For instance, in recipes containing maple syrup or honey, I've used such designations as locally produced or pure. In order to be designated organic, maple syrup producers must document that no pesticides or chemicals were used on the trees tapped or in the general area, that all the trees tapped were in good general health, and that all the sap used in production of the syrup can be traced to those sources. Since maple syrup by its nature is produced from forested maple trees, use of such substances may be minimal to begin with. I purchase maple syrup from my neighbor's small-scale organic farm, confident in the knowledge that even though their syrup may not specifically be labeled organic, I am getting a pure product, because I know their farming practices. Similarly, purchasing from a local, small-scale beekeeper assures me that I'm getting pure, pesticide-free honey. If you live in an area where locally produced maple syrup or honey is not readily available, looking for the organic designation will assure you that what you're getting is the real deal. However, you still need to be vigilant about reading labels carefully. For instance, I discovered organic "pancake syrup," which wasn't maple at all and contained, among other things, "organic caramel coloring," sitting side-by-side with pure organic maple syrup in a local store. As with so many other purchase decisions we make, it's wise to be an informed consumer.

Not having access to the large-scale supply of organic ingredients utilized by major producers of organic prepared foods can still prove a bit of a challenge. I've worked hard in formulating recipes for this cookbook to ensure the ingredients I used were as close to the real thing as I—or any other average person—could get. Sometimes that meant getting a little inventive, such as dicing up organic canned pineapple slices when I couldn't find crushed pineapple with the organic designation. And I've also made note of when a particular seasoning or other ingredient was not organic.

Please don't be discouraged if you cannot find every item in every recipe in organic form. Some organic is always better than none! You may even discover organic substitutions that suit you and your child just as well as the original version. Whether you're an old pro at organic cooking or just getting started, I hope you enjoy the variety you'll find in *The Organic Lunchbox*. And now, let's get started! Happy eating!

Breakfast for Lunch

Good Any Time of the Day

Breakfast foods have lots of kid appeal, and with a little planning can provide a tasty and balanced meal for lunch as well! When dealing with eggs, meat, or dairy, maintaining safe food temperatures is a must. The dishes here should all be sent safely chilled, in insulated containers or lunchboxes, with a frozen gel pack included. If your child's school has the facilities to reheat them, the egg and meat dishes can be warmed up there. If not, they're really not bad chilled, either.

Funny Face Bagels

Although I think of bagels as breakfast food, there are so many variations to these fun-to-make faces that you could enjoy them most any time of the day. Kids can easily construct their own funny faces, flowers, or whatever other design strikes their fancy in a matter of minutes.

Ingredients:
Organic bagels, split
Organic cream cheese, soy butter, or an alternative seed/tree nut
   butter, if allowed
Organic fruit spread, optional
Desired organic fruits and/or berries and/or vegetable slices
Shredded organic carrot or toasted organic coconut

Directions:
1) Spread each bagel half with the desired topping. If you'd like to add fruit spread, this can either be mixed in with the cream cheese, soy, seed, or nut butter, or smoothed on top of the bagel.
2) Next, add in sliced or whole fruits, berries, or vegetable slices to form your clown face of choice. Use a whole or half berry, cherry, or cherry tomato for the nose and grated carrot or toasted coconut for hair. One large half is probably plenty for a smaller child.
3) Place your completed clown face in a sandwich carrier, ready to be enjoyed for lunch! Keep it cool with a frozen gel pack until ready to eat.

Breakfast Burritos

I like soft corn tortillas for these simple sandwiches, although soft flour tortillas may be slightly less crumbly. Mixing together a bit of sour cream and yogurt makes a not-too-tangy kid-friendly condiment for spreading on each tortilla. Including a bit of Avocado Dip (p. 135) adds color, flavor, and nutritional value. You can easily use just the sour cream mixture or the avocado mixture, depending on your child's taste preferences.

Ingredients per burrito:
1 tablespoon sour cream
1 tablespoon plain Greek-style yogurt
1 Salsa Scrambled Egg (p. 11)
1 patty Slightly Spicy Sausage Patties (p. 12), optional
1 soft organic corn or flour tortilla
2 tablespoons Avocado Dip (p. 135)

Directions:
1) Combine the sour cream and yogurt, mixing well; set aside.
2) Prepare the Salsa Scrambled Egg as the recipe directs. Allow it to cool before constructing your burrito, unless it's being eaten right away.
3) Fry the sausage patty until it is evenly cooked; cut in half and cool before using. You could also crumble the sausage meat into the pan for cooking.
4) Spread one side of the tortilla with the sour cream/yogurt mixture and the Avocado Dip. Carefully place the egg (and sausage if using) in a line slightly to one side of the middle. Roll the tortilla up and wrap tightly in wax paper, twisting the ends shut. Add a paper towel wrap around the wax paper, if you wish.
5) Chill until serving time in an insulated lunchbox with a frozen gel pack. One end of the burrito can then be slowly unwrapped as lunch is enjoyed!

Savory French Toast Fingers

Breakfast doesn't have to be sweet in order to be tasty. Case in point is this savory version of French toast. You will note it is oven fried. It can be done on the stovetop if you prefer, but I think the more even heat of the oven helps keep the cheese from darkening too much while the French toast is cooking through. Depending on your kid's favorite flavor combinations, you can include a little container of ketchup, salsa, or marinara sauce (such as Italian Tomato Sauce, p. 95) for dipping purposes. Crispy Kale Chips (p. 123) or a little salad of string beans marinated in Italian or French dressing is also a nice accompaniment; breakfast can be as adventuresome as you wish it to be!

Makes 1 serving as listed; easy to multiply for more.

Ingredients per serving:
1 tablespoon organic oil
1 large organic egg
1 tablespoon organic milk
1 tablespoon organic grated Parmesan cheese
Pinch sea salt; about $1/8$ teaspoon
Organic black pepper, to taste
Pinch of organic basil or dry mustard, optional
Drop or two of hot sauce, optional
2 slices rustic-style organic bread

Directions:
1) Adjust your oven rack to the middle position, then preheat the oven to 375° F. Place the oil in a pan just large enough to hold the number of sticks you are preparing, making sure to coat the entire surface.
2) Beat together the egg and milk until smooth. Stir in the cheese, salt, pepper, and other desired seasonings.
3) Cut each slice of bread into 3–4 strips, removing a thin strip of crust if you wish to make them more even.
4) Dip both sides of each strip into the egg mixture, then place on the baking pan. Pour any extra egg mixture over the strips of bread. Bake for 10 minutes, then carefully insert a spatula under each "finger" and flip over, adding a bit more oil if necessary to prevent sticking. Bake for another 5 minutes, until golden brown.
5) Cool to room temperature before packing. Store in the refrigerator. Send to school with an iced gel pack to keep the egg component safely chilled.

Crunchy French Toast Fingers

One of the more disturbing kid meals I recall being served as breakfast for lunch when I worked in a local elementary school involved previously frozen French toast sticks that had been deep-fried in who knows what type of fat. They were accompanied by little tubs of dark, sticky syrup that bore no resemblance whatsoever to real maple syrup. I had a hard time equating this with a balanced lunch, although the kids seemed to love them. Here is a nice alternative; finger food–friendly French toast sticks with a mild, pure maple flavor. There is no need for sticky syrup here, although siding with fresh berries and some creamy yogurt makes for a tasty and healthy meal.

Makes 1–2 servings.

Ingredients:
¾ cup organic crispy rice cereal, finely crushed
¼ teaspoon organic cinnamon
1 large organic egg
2 tablespoons organic milk
1 tablespoon pure maple syrup
¼ teaspoon organic vanilla extract
Organic butter and organic coconut oil for frying
2–3 thick slices of organic bread

Directions:
1) Combine the crushed cereal and the cinnamon in a wide, shallow dish, then set it aside.
2) Beat the egg in another dish until the white and yolk are well combined. Stir in the milk, maple syrup, and vanilla.
3) Heat a heavy skillet or frying pan over medium heat; melt a bit of butter and coconut oil and spread to coat the entire surface of the pan.
4) Dip each piece of bread in the egg mixture, being sure to coat both sides. Then dip each side in the cereal crumbs, coating the bread completely. Sauté in the hot butter mixture, turning carefully once or twice during the process, until the bread is nicely browned on both sides and the egg is cooked through. Cut each slice into 3–4 "fingers" for serving.
5) Cool them to room temperature before storing for future lunches. Store them in the refrigerator in an airtight container so they stay nice and fresh. Send to school in an insulated container with an iced gel pack.

Apple Berry Sauce

Vary the types of berries used based on availability and personal taste. This recipe works fine with frozen berries as well as fresh; try stocking up on fresh, organic berries in season. Spread them on a baking sheet and quick-freeze them, then place in freezer storage bags and label for future use. Try combining two or more types of berries for a little variety. Store the sauce in the fridge, and send to school in leakproof containers.

Ingredients:

1 cup cored, peeled, diced organic apple
1 cup organic blueberries, raspberries, or diced strawberries
2 tablespoons locally produced honey
1 teaspoon organic cornstarch or potato starch

Directions:

1) Combine all ingredients in a small saucepan. Bring to a boil over medium heat, stirring constantly to prevent sticking.
2) Reduce heat and simmer for a couple of minutes to soften the fruit but still leave it fresh and bright.
3) Remove from heat and cool to room temperature before storing in the fridge.

Sopapillas with Apple Berry Sauce

Sopapillas are little fried biscuits that make a great alternative to commercially produced doughnuts. They contain considerably less sugar than the typical doughnut, and are accompanied by a tasty fruit sauce rather than overly sweet icing. The name translates as "sofa pillows," which you'll understand when you see their puffy shape once they're cooked. Send them to school dusted with just a bit of confectioners' sugar and a little container of Apple Berry Sauce (p. 8) for dipping purposes.

This recipe makes approximately 6 sopapillas.

Ingredients:
1 cup organic all-purpose flour
1 teaspoon organic sugar
½ teaspoon sea salt
2 teaspoons baking powder
2 tablespoons organic coconut oil
½ cup organic milk
Organic vegetable oil
Organic confectioners' sugar
Organic cinnamon, optional

Directions:
1) Combine the flour, sugar, salt, and baking powder. Crumble in the coconut oil until the mixture resembles coarse crumbs. Lightly stir in the milk.
2) Heat approximately 1 inch of oil in a small, heavy frying pan with the burner on the medium-high setting.
3) Pat out the dough to approximately 1 inch thick, then cut it into rectangles or squares. Trimming a narrow strip from each outer edge prior to cutting the dough will give you sopapillas that will puff up more evenly while frying.
4) Fry the sopapillas for 1–2 minutes per side, turning once, until they are evenly golden brown and cooked through. Drain on paper towels before dusting lightly with confectioners' sugar, then add a bit of cinnamon if you wish.
5) Cool to room temperature before packing in lunchboxes, and add a little container of Apple Berry Sauce for dipping them in.

Tip: This recipe can be adjusted to make more sopapillas if you wish. As with any fried bread, they are at their tastiest when eaten as fresh as possible.

Salsa Scrambled Eggs

This variation on scrambled eggs is so yummy, and yet so simple! It's an inexpensive and easy-to-eat way to fit some Tex-Mex flavor into your kid's lunchbox. As with any egg dish, keeping this southwestern-inspired scramble adequately chilled until lunch is imperative. Pack with a small frozen gel pack for safety's sake. You can easily prepare as many or as few of these as you wish.

Ingredients:
Large organic eggs
Per each egg:
1 tablespoon organic salsa
1 teaspoon organic butter
1–2 tablespoons shredded organic cheddar or jack cheese

Directions:
1) Beat the egg(s) with a fork until the whites and yolks are well blended. Stir in the salsa.
2) Melt the butter in a small cast-iron skillet or other heavy pan over medium heat.
3) Add the egg mixture to the pan and cook, gently sliding the firm eggs up over the uncooked portion until they are almost set. Sprinkle on the shredded cheese and fold over a few more times to finish cooking and to melt the cheese.
4) Allow to cool slightly before packing in a sealable lunch container or making into Breakfast Burritos (p. 4). Refrigerate until ready to pack for lunch. Send in an insulated lunch bag or box along with a frozen gel pack.

Slightly Spicy Sausage Patties

If your kiddo's taste runs to slightly spicier fare, try this sausage variation. It can be used and stored the same as Maple Sausage Patties (p. 13), but would also be tasty crumbled over a homemade pizza. As with the maple patties, look for humanely raised, antibiotic-free pork if you cannot find organically grown.

Makes 4–8 servings.

Ingredients:
1 pound ground pork
2 tablespoons water
1¼ teaspoons sea salt
½ teaspoon fresh ground organic black pepper
½ teaspoon paprika or smoked paprika
1 tablespoon organic cider vinegar
1 teaspoon fennel seeds, optional

Directions:
1) Combine all ingredients together in a bowl, mixing with a wooden spoon or your hands, until the mixture is totally combined.
2) Form into 8 thin, flat patties, or keep loose for crumbling over pizza. Dimpling one side of each patty with your fingertips will help the meat to retain its moisture when pan frying.
3) Cook the patties over medium heat until browned and cooked through.
4) Be sure to send them to school in an insulated container with a frozen gel pack, however you choose to use them.

Maple Sausage Patties

Sausage can be created with relatively few ingredients, although when produced commercially it often contains additives and preservatives. Organic pork is a rare commodity in my area; as an alternative, look for humanely raised, antibiotic-free meat. It's worth a trip to a specialty butcher if this is an option for you. Serve the sausage patties as an accompaniment to pancakes or waffles, or place a patty in a Baking Powder Biscuit (p. 156) or Whole Grain Slider Buns (p. 151) with cheese and/or an egg if you wish, to make a tasty breakfast sandwich. Be sure to keep it safe on the way to school in an insulated lunch container cooled with a frozen gel pack.

Makes 4–8 servings.

Ingredients:
1 pound ground pork
2 tablespoons pure maple syrup
1 tablespoon water
1¼ teaspoons sea salt
½ teaspoon fresh ground organic black pepper
2 teaspoons finely chopped organic sage, leaves only

Directions:
1) Mix all the ingredients together in a bowl, with your hands or a wooden spoon, until everything is thoroughly combined.
2) Form into 8 thin, flat patties. Dimpling the surface on one side with your fingertips will help the meat stay moist while frying.
3) Cook on each side over medium heat until browned and cooked through.

Tip: Uncooked patties can be placed on a baking sheet and frozen, then sandwiched between layers of wax paper, wrapped, and stored in the freezer for up to 1 month.

Green Eggs & Ham Breakfast Quiche

What kid doesn't know about green eggs and ham? Some children's classics never grow old! This savory quiche gets its unusual color from a combination of pureed peas and fresh herbs. If you cannot find organic ham, try using naturally cured ham or organic smoked turkey in place of the ham. If you prefer a vegetarian quiche, simply omit the meat and have a Green Eggs Quiche instead. I don't believe Dr. Seuss would mind in the least.

Makes 6 servings.

Ingredients:

1 9-inch unbaked Buttery Pie Crust (p. 21)
1½ cups frozen organic green peas
¾ cup organic vegetable or chicken broth
4 ounces organic cream cheese, softened
1 tablespoon minced fresh organic chives
1 tablespoon minced fresh parsley
½ teaspoon minced dried dill weed or
   1 teaspoon fresh

¼ teaspoon sea salt
⅛ teaspoon freshly grated nutmeg
4 large organic eggs
¾ cup organic milk
4 ounces diced organic or naturally cured ham
   or smoked organic turkey
4 ounces diced/shredded organic Swiss or
   mild cheddar cheese

Directions:

1) Make your pie crust dough and refrigerate while preparing the filling.
2) Place the peas and broth in a medium saucepan. Bring just to a full boil, then remove from heat and cool to room temperature; this is an important step, so you don't begin cooking the eggs in the filling until the quiche is actually in the oven.
3) In a blender or food processor, puree the peas and broth, then strain through a mesh strainer, smooshing down the pulp with a spoon to get as much of it through as possible while leaving the skins behind. This should yield about ¾ cup of puree.
4) Place the cream cheese and pea puree in the blender or food processor and blend until smooth. Add the minced herbs, salt, and nutmeg and blend until the mixture is smooth and creamy. Lastly, add in the eggs and milk, blending until smooth.
5) Sprinkle the diced ham and diced cheese evenly over the bottom of the unbaked pie crust. Gently pour the green eggs mixture over the ham and cheese.
6) Place the quiche in a preheated 425° F oven for 15 minutes. Reduce the heat to 350° F and continue baking for another 25–30 minutes, until the filling is evenly set. It should not be browned; this overcooking could toughen the filling or even make it watery. Remove from oven. If you wish, you can eat it right away, or allow it to cool for 1 hour and serve it at room temperature.
7) Immediately refrigerate the cooked quiche or any leftovers. Cut it into serving-size slices to fit into individual containers. Because of the egg content, send this to school in an insulated container with a frozen gel pack to keep it cool until lunch.

Multigrain Waffles

This recipe produces tender, fluffy waffles. Because a bit of maple syrup has been included right in the recipe, there's no need to send more along in your child's lunchbox; they taste just fine the way they are. Sunflower seeds can be added or not, as you wish.

This recipe yields 6–7 round Belgian-type waffles.

Ingredients:
¾ cup organic, whole wheat flour
¾ cup organic, unbleached white flour
¼ cup organic rolled oats
2 tablespoons ground flaxseed
4 teaspoons baking powder
½ teaspoon sea salt
¼ cup pure maple syrup
¼ cup organic vegetable oil or 5 tablespoons organic unsalted butter, melted
2 cups organic whole milk
4 large organic eggs
¼ cup hulled organic sunflower seeds, optional
Organic nonstick cooking spray

Directions:
1) Preheat your waffle iron.
2) In a medium mixing bowl, combine the flours, oats, flaxseed, baking powder, and salt. Add the sunflower seeds if desired. Stir until well blended.
3) Whisk together the maple syrup, oil or melted butter, milk, and eggs until the mixture is smooth and the yolks and whites have been thoroughly combined.
4) Add the wet ingredients to the dry ingredients, stirring just until well blended.
5) Spray the hot waffle iron with a bit of nonstick cooking spray each time you add batter to prevent sticking. Cook according to the waffle iron manufacturer's directions, keeping in mind that the darker batter may brown a bit faster than a standard waffle recipe.
6) Allow the waffles to cool thoroughly before packing into your preferred lunch containers. The cooked waffles can be wrapped or placed in lidded containers and refrigerated for a couple of days or frozen for up to 1 month.

Sweet Potato Pancakes

Golden Sweet Potato Puree helps make these pancakes moist and flavorful. They are sweet enough to eat as is, or consider some of the serving suggestions below. A small container of organic cottage cheese or a couple of Maple Sausage Patties (p. 13) would make protein-rich sides. The nutmeg adds a special flavor, but be aware that a little goes a long way, so aim for about a pinch of it when grating.

Makes approximately 1 dozen pancakes.

Ingredients:
⅔ cup organic milk
2 tablespoons melted organic butter
½ cup Golden Sweet Potato Puree (p. 143)
1 large organic egg
1 cup organic all-purpose flour
2 teaspoons baking powder
¼ teaspoon organic cinnamon
¼ teaspoon organic ginger
¼ teaspoon sea salt
Small grating of organic nutmeg
Desired toppings (see suggestions below)

Directions:
1) Whisk together the milk, butter, sweet potato puree, and egg until smooth. Combine the dry ingredients in a separate bowl. Add the dry ingredients to the wet ingredients, then stir to combine well.
2) Pour by the mixing spoonful into a hot, lightly oiled frying pan or skillet, turning once the top forms bubbles. Because the pancakes are fairly thick, make sure they are cooked through before removing from the pan.
3) Serve hot with choice of toppings, or allow to cool to room temperature before wrapping or packing and refrigerating. Be sure to keep them cool on the way to school.

Topping Options
These are tasty accompanied by a small dish of organic applesauce or Apple Berry Sauce (p. 8). You could also add a small container of Maple Honey Butter (p. 19) for spreading on at lunchtime, especially nice if the school allows kids to warm up their lunches.

Maple Honey Butter

Use this yummy spread on toast, pancakes, biscuits, or waffles. It's also great on non-lunch items, such as hot baked sweet potatoes or cooked squash, parsnips, even rutabaga or roasted onions!

This recipe makes 1 cup; approximately 16 servings

Ingredients:
1 stick organic butter, softened
¼ cup pure maple syrup
¼ cup locally produced honey
¼ teaspoon organic cinnamon, optional
½ teaspoon grated organic orange zest, optional

Directions:
1) Cream the butter, gradually adding in the maple syrup and honey until the mixture is light and fluffy. Stir in the cinnamon and/or orange zest, if desired.
2) Store, covered, in the fridge until ready to use. If you have several small containers, it may be easier to divide the butter mixture into individual-serving sizes before refrigerating. This will store well for 2–3 weeks.

Buttery Pie Crust

This easy-to-make pie crust can be used when making sweet or savory pies as well as quiche. You can even form leftover dough into Pie Crust Cookies (p. 201), Jam Roll-ups (p. 203), or Pie Crust Cheese Crackers (p. 161).

Makes enough dough for a generously apportioned single crust.

Ingredients:
¾ cup unbleached, all-purpose, organic flour
⅓ cup organic, whole wheat flour
¼ teaspoon sea salt
2 teaspoons organic brown sugar or turbinado sugar
6 tablespoons cold organic salted butter
2 ounces organic cream cheese
3–4 tablespoons cold water

Directions:
1) Combine the all-purpose flour, wheat flour, salt, and brown sugar in a blender or food processor. Cut the butter and cream cheese into chunks and add them in. Process or blend until it forms a fine crumb-like mixture. Add in the cold water, processing or blending just until the dough holds together. Note: If you want, you can cut the cream cheese and butter into the dry ingredients by hand, adding in the water and stirring with a fork until it just holds together.
2) Chill the dough for a few minutes to make it easier to handle.
3) Roll out on a lightly floured board and fit it loosely into a 9-inch pie plate, crimping the edges nice and high. Chill in the fridge while completing your filling.

Tip: If you have dough left over after making your crust, use it to make Pie Crust Cookies (p. 201) or Jam Roll-Ups (p. 203).

Tutti-Frutti Pancake Rolls

These tender pancake rolls are as colorful as they are delicious. Fresh or frozen fruits or berries will work in these, or use a combination. Cooking will be more even if the frozen fruit is at least partially thawed before adding it in; just don't let it get too mushy. Being fortunate enough to grow my own organic berries, I freeze them on trays in season and then store them in the freezer in resealable plastic bags. You can do this as well if you find a good buy on organic berries. Whole blueberries work fine for adding as is, but you will want to halve or quarter fruits such as raspberries and blackberries. Strawberries should be cut smaller still. Add in some diced apple or peaches for extra flavor and color, or even a bit of banana. Variety is the spice of life!

This recipe makes 6–7 pancake rolls.

Ingredients:

½ cup organic all-purpose flour
½ cup organic whole wheat pastry flour
1 tablespoon organic sugar
1½ teaspoons baking powder
½ teaspoon sea salt
½ teaspoon organic cinnamon
1 cup organic milk

1 large organic egg
2 tablespoons unsalted organic butter, melted, plus more for frying
1 teaspoon organic vanilla extract
1 cup diced mixed organic fruits and berries
Organic confectioners' sugar, pure maple syrup, Maple Nut Yogurt (p. 28), optional

Directions:

1) Place the flours, sugar, baking powder, salt, and cinnamon in a medium mixing bowl and whisk to combine.
2) Beat together the milk, egg, melted butter, and vanilla in a separate bowl. Pour the mixture over the dry ingredients and stir just until well combined.
3) Pour one 6-inch circle at a time onto a hot, lightly buttered griddle or skillet; cast iron is best. Sprinkle each pancake with a bit of the diced fruit. Fry until bubbles appear all over the surface; flip carefully to the other side and continue browning until the pancake is cooked through. If you're eating them right away, the cooked pancakes can be kept hot until all of them are ready by placing them on a baking sheet in a 350° F oven and covering them loosely with aluminum foil to prevent them from drying out.
4) I like to roll these pancakes into a long cylinder while they're still warm, then dust with a bit of confectioners' sugar just before eating. The cylinders also make for easy eating as a school lunch. Flip each pancake onto a wire rack to cool slightly before rolling and placing in a covered container in the fridge. You could send along a small container of pure maple syrup for dipping if you wish, although I think these are plenty sweet enough as is. Homemade Maple Nut Yogurt is an even better accompaniment; it's both tasty and nutritious. Make sure to send it chilled.

Sunny Side Up

When is an egg not an egg? When it's cottage cheese and fruit! When I was a kid, my mom sometimes fixed me a piece of toast topped with cottage cheese and pineapple, and I found it quite tasty. Organic cottage cheese with the pineapple already in it may be a challenge to find. If it's not available in your area, substitute plain cottage cheese and add a slice of organic pineapple along with half a peach or apricot; it will be just as tasty. Easy to prepare, fun to look at, and kid-friendly to eat, Sunny Side Up is a quick breakfast fix.

Makes 1 serving; easy to multiply for more.

Ingredients per serving:
½ cup organic cottage cheese with pineapple or plain organic cottage cheese
1 organic juice-packed canned peach or apricot half, well drained
1 slice organic pineapple if using plain cottage cheese

Directions:
1) Scoop the cottage cheese into your preferred serving container. If you're using plain cottage cheese, you may want to mix just a bit of the drained fruit juice into it for extra flavor.
2) Center the pineapple slice, if using, in the cottage cheese. Top it with the peach or apricot half.
3) Chill until lunch and send along a spoon or fork.

On the Side
Oatcakes (p. 163) or Homemade Graham Crackers (p. 159) make nice accompaniments to Sunny Side Up.

Teeny Tiny Tater Bites

Little mounds of crusty, shredded fried potatoes are another perennial kid favorite. However, some of the commercially produced ones contain additives no one wants or needs! This recipe is really quite simple, and will produce lovely little bites of potato-y goodness—crispy on the outside and tender within.

Makes 2–3 servings.

Ingredients:
2 cups shredded organic potatoes
¼ teaspoon sea salt
Dash of organic pepper
¼ cup organic olive oil
Organic ketchup or applesauce, optional

Directions:
1) Combine the potatoes, salt, and pepper, stirring to mix well. Drain off a bit of the excess moisture caused by the shredded potatoes interacting with the salt.
2) Heat 2 tablespoons of the oil in a cast-iron skillet over medium-high heat.
3) Drop the potato mixture by tablespoon-sized mounds into the hot oil. Cook until one side is golden, then flip and fry until the other side is also golden, at which time the Tater Bites should be cooked through. Remove and drain on a paper towel or parchment paper–lined baking sheet. Add more oil as necessary during the frying process.
4) Once they have cooled, pack in lunch containers, adding in a small container of organic ketchup, if you wish, for dipping. Some kids might prefer a little container of organic applesauce. Store in the refrigerator if prepared the night before.

Tip: If you're cooking a lot of Tater Bites at once and you plan to eat them right away, you can place the partially filled sheet in a 350° F oven to keep them warm until you're ready to serve them.

Pumpkin Yogurt

This is a yummy seasonal yogurt that's fun to make when pumpkins are ripe in your area. Because it utilizes pureed pumpkin, it has a smoother, creamier texture than many fruit yogurts. Please note that it is preferable to use homemade puree; canned pumpkin tends to be very compact and may affect the texture and flavor of this dish. If you wish, substitute Organic Sweet Potato Puree (p. 143) or even pureed butternut squash for the pumpkin.

Makes 3–4 servings.

Ingredients:
1 cup plain organic Greek-style yogurt
¼ cup organic pumpkin puree
2 tablespoons organic sugar or pure maple syrup
½ teaspoon organic cinnamon
½ teaspoon organic vanilla extract
⅛ teaspoon fresh grated organic nutmeg

Directions:
1) Combine all ingredients in a bowl. Stir together until well blended. Store, covered, in the refrigerator for up to 1 week.
2) Serve as is, or with some Homemade Graham Crackers (p. 159) as a special treat. It's also great for layering with granola and fruit, as in Autumn Pumpkin Parfaits (p. 37).

Maple Nut Yogurt

If your child's school is nut-free, you could try some of the walnut alternatives listed in the ingredients, or simply omit them altogether. Plain maple yogurt is a treat all in itself.

Makes 2–3 servings.

Ingredients:
1 cup plain organic Greek-style yogurt
3 tablespoons pure maple syrup
¼ cup toasted, chopped walnuts or roasted sunflower or pumpkin seeds

Directions:
1) To toast the walnuts, spread them on a baking pan and place in a preheated 350° F oven for approximately 5 minutes, until they are lightly browned and aromatic. They burn easily, so watch closely.
2) Combine the yogurt and maple syrup, stirring to blend well. Add the cooled walnuts or the seeds, again stirring to combine.
3) Store in the refrigerator in an airtight container.

Cornmeal Muffins

These muffins make a nice add-in to lunchboxes. Try including them with Salsa Scrambled Eggs (p. 11) for a tasty Breakfast for Lunch entrée, or pack to go with a smoothie. This is one of our kids' cooking club recipes; we enjoyed them with homemade soup! They can also serve as an accompaniment to salads or casseroles or stand by themselves at snack time.

Makes 12 muffins.

Ingredients:
12 paper baking cups or organic butter for pan
⅔ cup organic yellow cornmeal
6 tablespoons organic sugar or locally sourced honey
3 teaspoons baking powder
½ teaspoon sea salt
¼ cup melted organic butter
2 large organic eggs
1 cup organic milk

Directions:
1) Move the oven rack to the middle position, then preheat the oven to 375° F. Grease your muffin tin with butter or line with paper baking cups.
2) Combine the cornmeal, sugar, baking powder, and salt, then set aside.
3) Combine the melted butter and eggs, stirring until well combined. Add the milk, whisking lightly. Stir in the combined dry ingredients just until blended.
4) Pour the mixture evenly into the prepared muffin cups. Bake for 20–25 minutes, until lightly browned and springy to the touch. Serve warm or at room temperature with butter, jam, or just as they are.

Tip: If your child has a sweet tooth, try spreading with a bit of Maple Honey Butter (p. 19) as a tasty cupcake alternative.

Pumpkin Muffins

Include some cream cheese or a small chunk of cheddar for a little protein boost when sending sweet, mildly spicy Pumpkin Muffins for lunch. They are also a tasty add-on to cottage cheese and fruit, and they taste great with any chicken-, turkey-, or veggie-based soup. If you're in an area where sweet potatoes are more prevalent than pumpkins, try substituting Golden Sweet Potato Puree (p. 143) for the pumpkin in this recipe.

Makes 6 muffins.

Ingredients:
Paper baking cups, optional
Nonstick organic cooking spray or organic butter for the pan
1 cup organic all-purpose flour
½ teaspoon baking soda
½ teaspoon organic cinnamon
¼ teaspoon fresh grated organic nutmeg
¼ teaspoon organic ginger
¼ teaspoon sea salt
⅛ teaspoon ground organic cloves
4 tablespoons organic unsalted butter, melted
⅓ cup packed organic brown sugar
1 large organic egg
½ cup pureed organic pumpkin

Directions:
1) Preheat your oven to 375° F. Line 6 muffin cups with papers and/or coat with non-stick spray or brush with butter.
2) Combine the flour, baking soda, cinnamon, nutmeg, ginger, sea salt, and cloves in a medium bowl.
3) Stir together the melted butter and brown sugar. Beat in the egg and the pumpkin puree until well blended. Then, add the combined dry ingredients and stir together until smooth.
4) Divide the mixture evenly between 6 muffin cups that have been buttered or sprayed with organic nonstick spray. For ease of removal and serving, I like to use paper baking cups that I also lightly coat with nonstick spray before filling.
5) Bake for 25 minutes, until the muffins are mounded, cracked on top, and firm to the touch. Allow them to cool to room temperature before wrapping or packing for future use.

Tip: I use home pureed pumpkins. If you use canned pumpkin puree, it will probably be stiffer and have a lower moisture content. You may wish to decrease it by a tablespoon or two and add in a commensurate amount of water to get the right consistency in your batter.

Wild Blueberry Muffins

Living in northern New England, I'm fortunate to have easy access to wild blueberries. Blueberries in general contain lots of nutrients and antioxidants, and wild blueberries are even more packed with them than their domestic cousins. Try looking in your grocery freezer section for organic wild blueberries; they are frequently picked and packed right after harvest to retain their freshness. These muffins are sweet enough to pack as dessert as well as for a special breakfast or snack treat. When my older son turned six, I made blueberry muffins for him to share with his classmates rather than cupcakes; they were quite the hit. The buttery cinnamon topping is an optional bit of luxury.

Makes 12 muffins.

Ingredients:

12 paper baking cups
Nonstick organic cooking spray or melted organic butter for the pan
½ cup unsalted organic butter, softened
⅔ cup organic sugar
1 teaspoon organic vanilla extract
¼ teaspoon organic lemon extract, optional
¼ teaspoon fresh grated organic nutmeg
2 large organic eggs
1 cup organic pastry flour (regular or whole wheat)

¾ cup organic all-purpose flour
3 teaspoons baking powder
½ teaspoon sea salt
½ cup organic milk
2 cups organic wild blueberries, fresh or frozen

Optional topping:
1 teaspoon organic cinnamon
¼ cup organic sugar
¼ cup organic butter, melted

Directions:

1) Adjust your oven rack to the middle upper position, then preheat the oven to 375° F. Line muffin tins with the baking cups and coat with nonstick spray or brush with melted butter.

2) If the berries are frozen, place them in a strainer and run under cold water for a minute or two. Allow them to drain very well before using; a paper towel or piece of cheesecloth will help to absorb some of the excess liquid, if you wish.

3) Cream together the butter, sugar, vanilla, lemon extract, and nutmeg. Add in the eggs and beat well.

4) In a separate bowl, combine the flours, baking powder, and salt. Stir the combined dry ingredients and the milk into the butter mixture, beating until smooth and creamy. Then, gently fold in the blueberries.

5) Divide the mixture evenly between the muffin cups. Bake approximately 20–25 minutes; the tops should be mounded, lightly browned, and firm to touch. Serve warm or at room temperature.

6) For the optional topping, combine the cinnamon and sugar in a small bowl. Dip each muffin top quickly in the melted butter, and then dip into the cinnamon sugar.

7) Place in an airtight container for storage purposes; don't leave them in an overly warm or humid area.

Calico Muffins

The third graders and I used to make these in the fall, when there were plenty of apples, carrots, and zucchini for us to use. These moist, sweet muffins are rich enough to substitute for a dessert, yet full of all sorts of healthy and delicious ingredients.

Makes 18 muffins.

Ingredients:
18 paper baking cups or organic butter for pan
2 cups organic all-purpose flour
1 teaspoon organic cinnamon
1 teaspoon organic baking soda
½ teaspoon sea salt
1 teaspoon grated organic orange zest or lemon zest
2 large organic eggs
¾–1 cup organic sugar
¾ cup organic vegetable oil
1 teaspoon organic vanilla extract
1 cup shredded organic zucchini
1 cup shredded organic carrots
1 cup shredded organic red skinned apples
½ cup organic flaked coconut, optional
½ cup diced walnuts, optional

Directions:
1) Preheat your oven to 375° F. Line muffin tins with the baking cups or coat with butter.
2) Combine the flour, cinnamon, baking soda, salt, and zest in a medium bowl, then set aside.
3) Beat the eggs with a whisk or electric mixer until they are light and fluffy. Stir in the sugar, oil, and vanilla. Fold in the combined dry ingredients, then gently add in the zucchini, carrots, and apples. Fold in the coconut and/or nuts, if using.
4) Pour the mixture evenly into 18 the prepared muffin cups. Bake for 20–25 minutes, until the muffins are rounded, lightly browned, and firm to touch.

Tip: There is more sugar in these muffins than in many of the recipes in this book; they will average 2 teaspoons of sugar per muffin when using the full cup of sugar. The amount of sugar can be decreased slightly if you prefer, but the muffins will not be as tender.

Golden Granola

This is equally tasty as a breakfast cereal, for use in constructing Autumn Pumpkin Parfaits (p. 37), or for snacking out of hand. Even if your child's school does not allow peanuts or tree nuts due to allergy concerns, chances are you'll be all right with pumpkin seeds. If for some reason seeds are not allowed, simply leave them out of the recipe, it will still taste fine. You may also substitute pureed butternut squash or Golden Sweet Potato Puree (p. 143) for the pumpkin in this recipe.

Makes approximately 4 cups of granola; about 12 servings.

Ingredients:

¼ cup pumpkin puree
¼ cup pure maple syrup
¼ cup packed organic brown sugar
¼ cup organic vegetable oil
1 teaspoon organic cinnamon
½ teaspoon fresh grated nutmeg
¼ teaspoon organic allspice, optional

1 teaspoon grated organic orange or lemon zest
¼ teaspoon sea salt
3 cups organic rolled oats
½ cup roasted pumpkin seeds
¼ cup organic dried cranberries
¼ cup organic raisins

Directions:

1) Adjust your oven rack to the upper position, then preheat the oven to 350° F.
2) Combine the pumpkin, maple syrup, brown sugar, oil, spices, zest, and sea salt in a large bowl, whisking to combine well. Add in the rolled oats, stirring to completely coat them.
3) Turn out onto a parchment paper–lined baking sheet, spreading evenly. Bake for 25 minutes, then stir to redistribute evenly. Bake for another 25–30 minutes, stirring once or twice.
4) The granola should be lightly browned when it is done cooking. Remove from the oven and allow it to cool. Once it is at room temperature, stir in the pumpkin seeds, dried cranberries, and raisins. Store in an airtight container to preserve freshness.

Tip: The granola will burn more easily the closer to done it gets. Although it may still seem slightly moist after cooking, it should turn crisp and dry when slightly cooled. You can always pop it back in the oven for a few more minutes if you need to; this is an easier remedy than trying to salvage burnt granola if it stays in the oven for too long!

Autumn Pumpkin Parfaits

Berries, peaches, and mango are familiar choices when constructing fruit and yogurt parfaits. In this variation, juicy crisp apples or fresh fall pears combine with Pumpkin Yogurt and Golden Granola for a pleasing twist. A bit of orange or pineapple juice helps prevent browning of the fruit and adds a subtle splash of bright flavor.

Ingredients per serving:
¼ cup diced organic apples or pears
A bit of organic orange or pineapple juice
½ cup Pumpkin Yogurt (p. 27)
¼ cup Golden Granola (p. 36)

Directions:
1) Lightly coat the fruit with the orange or pineapple juice. You will not need very much juice at all, just a tiny bit to help keep the fruit from discoloring before it's time to eat.
2) If you're serving the parfaits at home, simply layer the yogurt, fruit, and granola in parfait glasses for a festive looking lunch.
3) When packing this for school it's better to keep the yogurt and fruit separate from the granola so the granola doesn't absorb the liquid and get all mushy. Since parfait glasses don't travel so well in a lunchbox, any leakproof lunch bowl will provide a perfectly serviceable receptacle for the fruit and yogurt, with a smaller container or sealable sandwich bag to hold the granola. Include a small ice pack to keep the fruit and yogurt nice and cool, and don't forget to pack a spoon!

Tip: For these parfaits, I prefer the fruit with the peel left on for both color and nutritional value. However, if you have a little person who really doesn't care for this, it's better to peel the fruit and have it eaten than to leave it as is and possibly have it end up in the school compost!

Double Oat Crunch Granola

Here's a granola variation that includes almost every kids' favorite cereal, crunchy little oat rounds, combined with the traditional granola standby of rolled oats. It's very versatile; fun for eating as is or layering with fruit and yogurt of choice. Try it in Cereal Sundaes (p. 41) as a fun Breakfast for Lunch entrée.

Makes 4 cups of granola.

Ingredients:
Organic nonstick cooking spray or organic oil
½ cup packed organic brown sugar
2 tablespoons organic vegetable oil
2 tablespoons organic apple cider or apple juice
¼ teaspoon sea salt
1 teaspoon organic vanilla extract
½ teaspoon organic cinnamon
2 cups organic oat rounds cereal (such as Cheerios)
1½ cups organic rolled oats

Directions:
1) Preheat the oven to 350°F. Coat a baking sheet with oil or nonstick cooking spray.
2) Combine the brown sugar, vegetable oil, apple cider, sea salt, vanilla, and cinnamon in a large, heavy saucepan. Bring to a boil over medium heat, stirring frequently to prevent burning. Remove from heat and immediately stir in the cereal and rolled oats.
3) Turn the mixture out onto the prepared baking sheet, then bake for 15–20 minutes, stirring once. The mixture should turn crispy but not browned. Remove from the oven, stir again, and allow to cool thoroughly
4) Store in an airtight container for up to 4 weeks. Send to school in a bowl-type container to be topped with milk just before eating, or combine with fresh berries and yogurt to make Cereal Sundaes.

Cereal Sundaes

Vary the serving size according to the size and appetite of the person eating it. Younger, tiny kids may require less than older, larger ones. This is an easy recipe for your children to put together independently. By placing the granola in a separate container, it can even be done the night before.

Makes 1 serving; easy to multiply for more.

Ingredients per serving:
¼–½ cup organic vanilla or Maple Nut Yogurt (p. 28)
¼–½ cup Double Oat Crunch Granola (p. 39)
¼–½ cup fresh or frozen, thawed organic raspberries, blueberries, blackberries, or sliced strawberries

Directions:
1) Place the yogurt in a sealable serving container, then top with the berries.
2) Send the granola along in a separate container for adding in just before eating. (Adding it earlier will result in soggy granola). Be sure to include a spoon!

Sandwiches, Soups & Salads

The Awesome Threesome for a Kid's Lunchbox

Soup and a sandwich has been a kid-friendly lunch staple for many generations of children. The increasing availability of fresh salad fixings adds a third favorite choice to the mix. Fortunately, insulated lunchboxes and reusable gel cold packs make cold salads and sandwiches both safe and appetizing lunch choices. In the case of hot soups, use a reliable thermos, following the manufacturer's instructions carefully to maintain optimal temperatures until lunchtime. I suggest you visit the Safety.com website (safety.com/blog/how-to-select-and-safely-use-a-thermos) for further information on safe handling of hot and cold lunch foods.

Classic Mini Pizzas

As with the Apple Mini Pizzas (p. 46), once cooled these can easily be stored by either wrapping individually or placing in a covered container and storing in the fridge for 2–3 days. I wouldn't recommend longer than this as the sauce may cause them to become rather soggy with time. If your child has access to a microwave in the lunchroom, these will warm up nicely; otherwise they are just fine at room temperature.

Ingredients:
Organic English muffins, split (I prefer whole wheat)
Organic pizza or marinara sauce (see Italian Tomato Sauce recipe on p. 95 if you prefer homemade)
Shredded mozzarella cheese
Optional toppings:
Diced organic bell peppers
Organic olives
Sliced, lightly cooked organic carrot slices
Grated organic Parmesan cheese

Directions:
1) Adjust your oven rack to the upper level, then preheat the oven to 400° F.
2) Place the desired number of English muffin halves, cut side up, on a baking sheet. Spread each half with a thin layer of the sauce—thick enough to give a nice serving, but not too thick or it will seep into the muffin. Top with a generous sprinkling of the mozzarella. Add on the optional toppings, if you wish. I stick to fairly small toppings that are not too moist.
3) Bake until the cheese bubbles nicely but does not brown, about 7–10 minutes.
4) Cool completely before wrapping or placing in your serving container; refrigerate for safekeeping until ready to send for lunch.

Apple Mini Pizzas

This is an easy recipe to make in advance, especially since the pizzas should cool before wrapping them to prevent the cheese from sticking. If you make enough for 2–3 days' worth of lunches, you can store them in a covered container in the fridge (put a piece of waxed paper between slices), or you can simply individually wrap them so they're all set to pop in a lunchbox! Just be sure to wrap them airtight, so they don't become stale and hard.

Ingredients:
Organic English muffins, split
Favorite organic fruit spread
Thinly sliced organic apples
Cinnamon
Shredded organic cheddar cheese

Directions:
1) Adjust your oven rack to the upper level, then preheat the oven to 400° F.
2) Place the desired number of English muffin halves on a baking sheet with the cut side up. Spread each half with a thin layer of fruit spread. Top with the apple slices and sprinkle lightly with cinnamon. Add a small mound of the shredded cheese to top each.
3) Bake until the cheese bubbles nicely but does not brown, about 7–10 minutes.
4) Cool completely before wrapping or placing in your serving container. Store in the refrigerator if made in advance.

Cheese Quesadillas

This recipe is about as easy as they come, and very tasty, too. Cut the tortilla rounds into wedges while still warm, and then allow them to cool before packaging for lunch. Include a little container of salsa and/or Avocado Dip (p. 135) for dunking the quesadilla triangles.

Ingredients:
Organic corn or wheat soft tortillas
Shredded organic cheddar or Monterey Jack cheese
Organic nonstick cooking spray, vegetable oil, or organic butter
Avocado Dip (p. 135) and/or your favorite organic salsa

Directions:
1) For each quesadilla, use two soft tortillas. Place a generous amount of shredded cheese on one, then place it carefully on a lightly oiled, buttered, or sprayed hot skillet.
2) Cook on one side until the cheese begins to melt. Top with the other tortilla, pressing down lightly. Carefully turn and cook on the other side until the filling is just melted through; it's better not to overcook the cheese or it will be tough when it cools. The tortillas should be lightly browned at this point.
3) Remove to a cutting board and cut into 6–8 wedges, depending on the size of the tortillas.
4) Allow them to cool, then place in sandwich or other containers and refrigerate until it's time to send them for lunch. Include the desired condiments in small separate containers.

Tip: A heavy cast-iron skillet or griddle will work best for this recipe, as iron distributes the heat more evenly, especially at high temperatures.

Grilled Cheese Roll-ups

Here's a fun way to vary your grilled cheese sandwiches. These cheesy little cylinders make great kid-sized finger food, and are so convenient for dipping into hot soup! Soft white bread works best for this recipe, so that your roll-ups don't end up cracking when you construct them. Removing the crusts also facilitates easy roll-up and even browning.

Plan on 1–2 roll-ups per serving.

Ingredients per roll-up:
1 slice organic soft white bread
Organic yellow mustard, optional
2–3 tablespoons shredded organic cheese
Thin spears of organic dill pickles or organic pimento stuffed olives, optional
Organic butter for grilling

Directions:
1) Begin by trimming a thin slice of crust away from each edge of the bread. Use a rolling pin to roll the bread as flat as you can get it; it may try to spring back up on you!
2) Spread one side only with a bit of mustard, if you wish. It will add flavor and also helps the cheese to stick until it has a chance to melt and adhere to the bread.
3) Sprinkle the cheese evenly over the top of the slice, leaving about ½-inch margin on each side. If you wish, position a thin spear of pickle or a row of olives just off center, on top of the cheese. Roll the bread up tightly, starting on the side nearest the pickle/olives, placing each roll-up seam side down when you are done.
4) Place a skillet or frying pan over medium heat. Note: Browning these sandwiches works best if you have a heavy cast-iron skillet or frying pan that will conduct the heat evenly throughout your roll-ups. Melt a little butter in a thin line about as wide as the cheese roll-up. Place each roll-up, seam side down, in the hot butter. Allow the sandwich to grill until the cheese around the seam line has melted and "glued" the sandwich shut. Adding more butter to the pan as you progress, roll the sandwiches over to brown them evenly on all sides.
5) Allow the roll-ups to cool to room temperature before packing for lunch. If storing overnight, place in the refrigerator.

Alternate method: You can place the open slice of bread in a thin pool of the hot melted butter before adding the cheese and rolling up. This helps the cheese adhere without using mustard, but it is a bit hazardous to roll up due to the heat, and therefore also doesn't roll as tightly. If you choose this technique, the roll-up will still need to continue to brown in the butter until golden on all sides.

Cracker Stackers

There seems to be a plethora of cracker, cheese, and meat grab-and-go lunches readily available in most stores. While they're certainly convenient and kid-friendly, as balanced lunches go they are definitely lacking. Using a little ingenuity, you can substitute more varied and wholesome ingredients for your child to construct her/his own "cracker stackers." A sectioned lunch container works well for holding each part of the stackers separately until your kiddo assembles them at lunchtime. Send in an insulated lunchbox with a frozen gel pack for cooling. If you want to make them particularly appealing, try investing in some cracker-sized cookie cutters for trimming slices of meat, cheese, or veggies into rounds, stars, or flowers; this is sure to be a hit with the junior set. They'll soon be the envy of the school lunch bunch!

Turkey Cracker Stackers
Ingredients:
Organic crackers of preference
Thinly sliced organic Swiss or mild cheddar cheese, cut into cracker-sized serving sections
Organic cooked turkey, thinly sliced and cut into cracker-sized serving sections
Organic jellied cranberry sauce, sliced and cut into cracker-sized serving sections

Directions:
1) Place each component in its own little section. Crackers can fit right in as well, or keep them separate for freshness.

Mozzarella Cracker Stackers
Ingredients:
Organic crackers of preference
Organic mozzarella cheese, sliced and cut into cracker-sized serving sections
Organic plum tomatoes, thinly sliced
Edamame Pesto (p. 142) or Traditional Pesto (p. 142)

Directions:
1) Make sure the tomato slices and pesto stay separate from the cheese and crackers, otherwise they could become soggy. Add in a little spoon for dishing out the pesto.

Egg-stra Tasty Cracker Stackers
Ingredients:
Organic crackers of preference
Egg Salad Sandwich Filling (p. 53) or Tofu Salad Sandwich Filling (p. 58)
Organic cucumber slices

Directions:
1) Use a well-sectioned container, or send the egg or tofu filling in their own lidded container and the crackers separate from the cucumber slices so that everything stays nice and crisp until it's time to eat. Remember to include a small spoon for spreading the filling on the crackers.

Tuna Salad Sandwich Filling

Although for many years tuna was considered a healthy and kid-friendly sandwich filling, in more recent times concerns about mercury and other contaminants have made it seem less appealing. If you're interested in finding out which tuna brands are rated the safest, and why, I suggest going to Greenpeace's 2015 Canned Tuna Guide (www.greenpeace.org/usa/oceans/tuna-guide). Unfortunately, none of the familiar, widely distributed brands make it anywhere near the top. A few of the picks from this site include Wild Planet, American Tuna, Ocean Naturals, Whole Foods, Hy-Vee, and Trader Joe's. Once you've determined which tuna to purchase, it can be put to good use making this Tuna Sandwich Filling.

Makes enough for 2 sandwiches.

Ingredients:
5–6.5 ounces water-packed tuna
2 tablespoons finely diced organic celery
2–3 tablespoon organic mayonnaise.
1–2 tablespoons organic pickle relish, optional

Directions:
1) If the tuna is from a can, drain well. The packets are generally sealed with very little extra liquid, so no draining is necessary if that's what you are using.
2) Flake the tuna with a fork, add the celery, mayonnaise, and pickle relish, if desired, and stir to combine well.
3) Use for sandwiches, mini sliders, Under the Sea Salad (p. 79), or just send it in a little container to enjoy as is. Be sure to send with a frozen gel pack to keep the tuna nice and cold until lunchtime.

Egg Salad Sandwich Filling

Egg salad is one of those classic fillings that is economical, versatile, and a perennial kid favorite. Organic eggs are readily available and are an easy way to boost your child's protein intake. Celery and parsley add color, flavor, and a tiny nutritional boost. Plan on one egg for each mini slider or set of Egg-Stra Tasty Cracker Stackers (p. 51), two for a full-sized sandwich. This is easy to multiply by as many eggs as you'd like.

Makes enough for 1 large or 2 small sandwiches.

Ingredients:
2 organic eggs
2 tablespoons finely diced organic celery
½ teaspoon organic parsley flakes, or 1 teaspoon fresh minced
2–3 tablespoons organic mayonnaise
Sea salt and organic black pepper, to taste
Sliced organic olives, optional

Directions:
1) Hard boil the eggs by placing them in cold water in a covered saucepan. Bring just to boiling, then immediately turn off the heat, but leave the pan on the burner. Leave the eggs, covered, to cook for 10 minutes.
2) Drain off the hot water, then cover the eggs with cold water. Change the water a couple of times to bring them quickly to room temperature. Once they're at room temperature, the eggs can be peeled or placed in the refrigerator.
3) Chop or mash the cooled, peeled eggs as fine as you'd like, adding in the celery, parsley, mayonnaise, salt, and pepper. If desired, add in the olives now or sprinkle them over the filling when constructing your sandwiches.
4) Place in tightly covered container to prevent discoloring. Remember to keep any egg dish very cool prior to consuming; an insulated lunch bag or lunchbox with frozen gel pack is the way to go. Use the hard-boiled eggs or egg salad within 2–3 days.

Tip: For easier peeling, tap the eggs on a hard surface to crack the peel all over while they're sitting in the cooling water. This enables some liquid to enter in between the egg membrane and the cooked egg white, making it easier to peel off the shell.

Tiny Turkey Sliders

These little sandwiches taste best when they're nice and fresh, although they can easily be prepared the night before and stored in the fridge until it's time to leave for school. Make as many as the size and appetite of your child dictates.

Makes 4 sliders; about 2 servings.

Ingredients:
¼ cup organic mayonnaise
2 tablespoons organic canned cranberry sauce
Preferred slider buns, purchased, or Whole Grain Slider Buns (p. 151)
Cooked, sliced organic turkey
Organic Swiss or provolone cheese slices or other cheese of choice, optional
Thinly sliced organic tomato, optional
Organic lettuce, well washed and patted dry

Directions:
1) Combine the mayonnaise and cranberry sauce in a small bowl. Spread some on each side of the split bun.
2) Layer on the sliced turkey, cheese, tomato, and lettuce. Top with the other half of the bun, then wrap or place in a sandwich container. Add a small frozen gel pack to the lunchbox to keep the sliders properly cool until lunchtime.

Mini Meatloaf Sliders

Here's one nifty way to use our little meatloaf or beet loaf cupcakes—just make sure to omit the mashed potato frosting from any designated for these sliders! I prefer dill pickle relish for the sandwich spread, but feel free to use the relish of your choosing. One of these will probably be enough for a very small child, although older kids could probably eat two or three.

Makes 4 sliders; about 2 servings.

Ingredients:
¼ cup organic mayonnaise
1 tablespoon organic ketchup
1 tablespoon organic pickle relish, well drained
Meatloaf Cupcakes (p. 93) or Beet Loaf Cupcakes (p. 91), unfrosted
Preferred slider buns, purchased or Whole Grain Slider Buns (p. 151)
Organic lettuce, well washed and patted dry
Organic cheddar cheese slices or other cheese of choice, optional

Directions:
1) Combine the mayonnaise, ketchup, and pickle relish in a small bowl; set aside.
2) Cut each mini meatloaf or beet loaf in half horizontally. Slice each bun in half horizontally if they haven't already been split.
3) Spread some of the mayonnaise mixture on each bun half and layer on half a meatloaf or beet loaf cupcake, lettuce, and a small slice of cheese, if you wish. Replace the tops of the buns and wrap securely with wax paper, parchment paper, or foil, or place in a reusable sandwich container. Send with a frozen gel pack to keep them properly chilled.

Chicken Rice Soup

This is one of the recipes we made during our after-school kid's cooking club. It's especially easy to concoct using leftover roasted organic chicken or turkey. Some choice options are suggested in the ingredients list. The dried cranberries add an especially nice brightness to the soup, both with color and flavor.

Makes 8 servings.

Ingredients:
2 cooked chicken thighs, leftover roasted/rotisserie chicken, or a turkey drumstick
6 cups organic chicken broth
2 cups water
2 stalks organic celery, thinly sliced
1½ cups organic carrots, sliced thin
½ cup diced organic onion or 2 tablespoons organic instant minced onion
2 teaspoons organic dried parsley
1 organic bay leaf, optional
½ cup uncooked organic white rice
1 cup frozen organic peas
Dried organic cranberries
Sea salt and organic pepper, to taste

Directions:
1) Pull the chicken or turkey meat off the bones and break into bite-sized pieces.
2) Combine everything except the peas, cranberries, salt, and pepper in a large pan, adding in the chicken bones and skin for more flavor. Bring to a boil, then reduce the heat and simmer for approximately 15 minutes, until the rice is tender and the vegetables are cooked.
3) Add the peas and salt and pepper to taste. Cook about 5 minutes longer.
4) Remove the skin, bones, and bay leaf before serving.
5) If you wish, sprinkle a few dried cranberries over each bowl of soup just before eating. For school lunches, pour the piping hot soup into a reliable thermos, adding a small container of the dried cranberries to sprinkle over when it's time to eat.

Tofu Salad Sandwich Filling

Tofu makes a tasty vegan substitute for egg salad if you prefer to forego eggs. If you are not vegan, regular organic mayonnaise can easily be substituted for the vegan variety.

Makes enough for 2–3 sandwiches.

Ingredients:
1 cup (4 ounces) firm organic tofu, diced
¼ cup diced organic celery
2 tablespoons finely shredded organic carrot
1 tablespoon minced organic chives or scallions
¼ teaspoon sea salt
Few grinds organic black pepper
1 teaspoon organic yellow mustard
2–3 tablespoons organic mayonnaise (vegan or regular)

Directions:
1) Place all the ingredients in a small mixing bowl, stirring well to combine. The diced tofu will resemble hard-cooked egg whites once the Tofu Salad is completed.
2) Refrigerate until ready to pack for lunch and send with a frozen gel pack to keep it cool. Use in sandwiches, on crackers as in Cracker Stackers (p. 51), or enjoy it as is.

Fish Stick Tacos

In trying to research whether ocean fish can be classified as organic, I came across quite a bit of information, but not too many definitive answers. The original guidelines formulated in 1993 indicated wild caught fish might be categorized as such. From what I've been able to ascertain, there doesn't currently seem to be certified organic wild-caught fish harvested from US waters. However, in general, the United States, Canada, and parts of Australia are considered to be some of the best sources for clean seafood in the world. West Coast seafood from the US and Canada was consistently mentioned as a source for safe, sustainably harvested fish. There is also a movement heading in the direction of granting organic status to certain farmed fish. Additionally, the Marine Stewardship Council grants certification to companies or organizations that harvest farmed or responsibly wild-caught fish in a manner that can be traced back to sustainable sources. Look for the blue MSC label when purchasing fish sticks or other fish products.

Fish Stick Tacos are easy to prepare the night before. Once the fish sticks have cooled to room temperature, refrigerate for safekeeping. Be sure to send them in an insulated container with a chilling agent, such as a frozen gel pack, as fish in general is very perishable.

Makes 4 servings.

Ingredients:
1 cup finely shredded organic cabbage
2 tablespoons organic mayonnaise
1 tablespoon finely minced organic dill pickle or pickle relish
1 teaspoon minced organic chives, optional
8–12 fish sticks
Organic corn or flour soft taco shells

Directions:
1) Combine the shredded cabbage with the mayonnaise, pickle, and chives; set aside.
2) Cook 2-3 fish sticks per taco according to the directions on the box. Cool to room temperature before assembling tacos.
3) Place fish sticks and about ¼ cup of the cabbage mixture on each taco shell. Fold the shell over, then wrap in waxed paper or parchment paper for easy eating later on. Alternatively, place the cabbage mixture in a small sealed bowl and send the wrapped fish sticks and taco shells separately, so the fish tacos can be constructed just before eating them—there's less chance of a soggy taco that way!
4) Place in an insulated lunch container and make sure to send with a frozen cooling pack . . . and an extra napkin or two.

Open-Faced Rice Cake Sandwiches

These are almost as much fun to create as they are to eat! It's easy to let your kids make their own; simply put out dishes of prepared vegetables, rice cakes, and your preferred spreads. Fitting them into a sandwich container will help keep the sandwiches level until lunchtime. Here are some suggestions to get you started.

Ingredients:
Organic rice cakes
Choice of spreads:
Sunflower seed butter or soy butter
Plain cream cheese
Deb's Pink Radish Dip (p. 141)
Avocado Dip (p. 135)
Easy Cheese Spread (p. 137)
Choice of fresh organic veggies:
Baby carrots or carrot slices
Cucumbers
Broccoli florets
Radishes
Bell peppers
Celery
Cherry tomatoes
Mushrooms
Zucchini
Summer squash

Directions:
1) Spread the flatter side of each rice cake with a thin layer of your desired spread.
2) Add on the veggies of choice to make a picture, a design, or just to pile on lots of garden goodness!
3) Send to school in a covered sandwich container or flat-bottomed salad bowl with a lid. If using dairy products as part of the spread, it's a good idea to add in a chilled gel pack to keep things cool and crisp.

Broccoli Cheese Soup

Broccoli and cheese is such a yummy combination! It might just be a good way to help a kid who doesn't like broccoli to discover that she/he does, after all. It fills you right up on a cold winter day.

Makes 3–4 servings.

Ingredients:
2 cups diced organic broccoli
1 cup organic broth of choice
Approximately 1¼ cups organic milk
2 tablespoons organic butter
2 tablespoons organic cornstarch or potato starch
¼ teaspoon sea salt
¼ teaspoon dry mustard
⅛ teaspoon fresh grated organic nutmeg
Dash white pepper, optional
1 cup shredded organic cheddar cheese

Directions:
1) Combine the diced broccoli and broth in a small saucepan. Cover, bring to a boil, and cook until the broccoli is just tender but still nice and bright green. Drain the cooking liquid into a 2-cup liquid measuring cup, then add enough milk to equal 2 cups.
2) Melt the butter in a medium saucepan, then stir in the starch and cook over medium heat for a minute or two; be careful not to brown too much.
3) Stir in the salt, dry mustard, nutmeg, pepper, and milk mixture; whisk and heat to a boil.
4) Add in the broccoli and cheddar cheese, heating again just until the cheese melts. Your soup is now ready to serve or cool and store for lunch another day.

Tip: Dicing the broccoli fine will produce an easier-to-eat soup.

Oodley Noodley Soup

Those little round pasta shapes are always popular with the elementary school set. In this soup, there are plenty to go around! Of course, if organic pasta rounds are elusive in your neck of the woods, a different pasta can always be substituted. Vary the amounts of peas and corn used depending on how vegetable-oriented your kiddos are.

Makes 4–5 servings.

Ingredients:
4 cups organic chicken broth or stock
1 cup water
4 ounce organic or natural boneless, skinless chicken breast
1 tablespoon dried organic onion flakes
1 teaspoon organic parsley flakes
¼ cup thinly sliced organic celery
¼ cup finely diced organic carrots
1 clove organic garlic, peeled and halved
1 cup uncooked organic O- shaped pasta
¼ –½ cup organic corn (loose pack frozen works well)
¼—½ cup organic peas or green edamame (loose pack frozen works well)
Sea salt
Fresh ground organic black pepper

Directions:
1) Dice the chicken into ¼-inch cubes.
2) Combine everything except the corn, peas, salt, and pepper in a large saucepan. Bring to a boil, then reduce the heat and boil gently for 10–15 minutes.
3) Add the corn and peas, return to boiling, then reduce the heat and simmer another 10 minutes, until everything is done to your liking. Taste for seasoning, adding a bit of sea salt and pepper if desired.
4) Remove the garlic before pouring piping hot into lunch thermoses, or cool and refrigerate for another day.

Alphabet Vegetable Soup

The after-school cooking club kids enjoyed this tasty vegetable soup featuring tiny pasta. If you cannot find organic alphabet pasta, any tiny variation will do. I've found that star-shaped pasta works quite well. Depending on the type of broth used, this can be made vegetarian or not.

Makes 6–8 servings.

Ingredients:
6 cups organic vegetable, beef, or chicken broth
15-ounce can organic diced tomatoes
½ cup diced onion or 2 tablespoons organic instant minced onion
1 cup diced organic red-skinned potatoes
2 cups frozen mixed organic vegetables
2 organic bay leaves, optional
1 teaspoon Italian mixed herbs
1 tablespoon organic sugar or locally sourced honey
2 tablespoons organic butter or margarine
1 cup uncooked organic alphabet pasta or other tiny pasta
½ teaspoon sea salt
Dash of organic pepper, to taste

Directions:
1) Combine everything except the butter, pasta, salt, and pepper in a large saucepan. Bring to a boil, reduce the heat, and simmer, covered, for 10–15 minutes, until the potato is barely cooked and the vegetables are tender.
2) Stir in the butter and pasta and cook about 10 more minutes.
3) Pour the hot soup into a preheated thermos for school lunch and serve with your sandwich of choice.

Easy Creamy Tomato Soup

Be sure to use tomato paste in this recipe rather than sauce, which is not as concentrated and frequently contains ingredients other than tomatoes. Organic vegetable stocks and broths can vary widely in flavor. I prefer using Emeril brand in this particular soup, as I think it has a nice blend of vegetable flavors with a little underlying sweetness that combines well with the tomato. Product availability and individual taste may dictate your stock of prefer-ence. This soup can be made in its classic dairy form with the addition of whole milk, or you can use vegetable stock only and substitute your favorite vegetable-based spread instead of butter for a creamy vegan version.

Makes 3 servings (easy to double).

Ingredients:
3 tablespoons organic butter
3 tablespoons organic flour or cornstarch
1¾ cups organic vegetable stock
6 tablespoons organic tomato paste
1 tablespoon organic sugar or locally sourced honey
1 cup organic whole milk or 1 additional cup organic vegetable stock
¼ teaspoon organic paprika
Few shakes pepper sauce, optional

Directions:
1) In a medium saucepan, melt the butter over medium heat. Stir in the flour or cornstarch and allow the mixture to cook for a minute or two, stirring constantly so that it doesn't brown. This step is important so that your soup doesn't retain an "uncooked flour" flavor.
2) Whisk in the 1¾ cups of vegetable stock and bring to a boil, whisking frequently to prevent lumps from forming.
3) Add in the tomato paste and sugar and cook 1 minute longer.
4) Reduce the heat and stir in the milk or additional stock, paprika, and the pepper sauce, if using. Heat to just under boiling (boiling could result in curdling or burn-ing of the soup).
5) Ladle your nice hot soup into a pre-warmed thermos for safe passage to school. Store cooled leftovers, covered, in the refrigerator. This soup goes exceedingly well with Grilled Cheese Roll-ups (p. 49).

Tomato Rice Soup

Tomato rice soup is vegetarian-style comfort food for the young and not-so-young alike. If you prefer, chicken broth may be used instead of vegetable. I personally really like the chicken-less broth sold under the Imagine organic label for this recipe. I use this broth in a wide variety of dishes. The tiny dash of balsamic vinegar in this recipe adds a subtle hint of flavor. You can also substitute 1 teaspoon each of cider vinegar and honey if you don't have any balsamic on hand.

Makes 4–5 servings.

Ingredients:
¼ cup diced onion
2 tablespoons organic butter
3 cups peeled, seeded, chopped organic plum tomatoes
3 cups organic vegetable or chicken broth
3 tablespoons organic jasmine rice
1 organic bay leaf
1 teaspoon balsamic vinegar
Sea salt to taste
Organic black pepper to taste

Directions:
1) Sauté the onion in the butter in a medium saucepan until tender but not browned.
2) Add the tomatoes, broth, rice, bay leaf, and vinegar. Bring just to a boil, then reduce heat and simmer for about 30 minutes, until the tomatoes and rice are very soft and cooked through.
3) Taste and add a few grinds or shakes of sea salt and pepper to season as you wish. Remove the bay leaf before serving.
4) Cool the soup before storing it in the fridge; bring back just to boiling before pouring into thermoses for school. This soup is especially tasty with tuna or grilled cheese sandwiches.

Carrot Surprise Soup

The surprise in this creamy carrot soup is . . . soy or nut butter! It enriches, thickens, and adds mellow flavor to the carrot base. The extra protein also makes it a good nutritional choice for vegetarian or vegan kids. I have found soy butter to be a bit drier than other nut or seed butter, so if you use it in this recipe you may wish to add just a bit of oil or dairy butter for smoother texture and enhanced flavor. If your school allows (and your child can tolerate) tree nuts, cashew butter is a delicious choice for this recipe. Sun butter is another good alternative. If for some reason the school doesn't allow any of the above, better save your soup for a satisfying at-home lunch on a damp, rainy day.

Makes 4 servings.

Ingredients:
2½ cups diced organic carrots
3 cups organic vegetable broth
¼ cup organic cashew, sunflower seed, or soy butter
1–2 teaspoons organic butter or oil (see above note), optional
½ teaspoon organic cinnamon
¼ teaspoon organic ginger
Desired toppings, see below for suggestions

Directions:
1) Cook the carrots in a medium saucepan, tightly covered, in the broth until they are very tender, about 20 minutes, adding a bit of water if necessary to keep the liquid levels even.
2) Add in the cashew, soy, or sunflower seed butter (and the butter or oil, if using soy butter) along with the spices, and then combine in a blender or food processor until the soup is creamy and smooth.
3) Although this is not as perishable as soups with meat or poultry added, it should be refrigerated until just before lunches are sent. At that point, heat it to just under boiling so that it will stay nice and hot in the thermos. It is also not half bad served at room temperature, if you prefer to go that route.

Suggested Toppings
Shredded organic carrots, organic raisins, and/or roasted soybeans/cashews/sunflower seeds all make tasty toppings for this soup. Or you could try adding some of those cute little bunny crackers. We all know rabbits love carrots!

Rainbow Chard Salad

When my kids were little, we used to enjoy a fresh spinach salad I made with creamy dressing and crisp bacon crumbled over the top. This colorful version uses rainbow chard instead of spinach, although organic spinach can be substituted if there's no chard available. It features a variety of possible toppings and add-ins. It can be assembled in advance if you want to keep things simple, although the chard will hold its crispness better if the dressing and toppings are added just before eating. Either way, it tastes delicious!

Makes 4 kid-sized servings.

Ingredients:
¼ cup organic mayonnaise
1 tablespoon organic cider vinegar
2 tablespoons locally sourced honey or organic agave nectar
Pinch of organic dill weed, optional
¼ teaspoon organic onion powder
10 ounces organic rainbow chard, well rinsed and shaken mostly dry
¼ cup organic raisins
4 slices naturally cured bacon, cooked and crumbled, or ¼ cup toasted, salted sunflower
    seeds or pine nuts
2 sliced hard-boiled organic eggs, optional
1 organic orange, sectioned, optional
½ cup organic Swiss or mild cheddar cheese, optional

Directions:
1) Whisk together the mayonnaise, vinegar, honey, dill weed, and onion powder to make the dressing.
2) If using separate lunch bowls, divide the chard evenly between 4–5 bowls, or place in one large bowl if combining everything at once.
3) Stir the dressing lightly into the salad, and then add the desired toppings. If sending to school, I recommend that you send the dressing and toppings in small, separate containers to be added just before eating.

Tip: This salad is hearty enough to serve as the main course if you wish, accompanied by some good quality bread and butter.

Kiddie Fruit Salad

When I first began working with primary-level kids a number of years ago, there was a kindergarten teacher named Anne who regularly served her class this colorful tri-fruit salad. It was a great way to brighten up a gloomy fall or winter day. Let your child's taste and your school's dietary restrictions help dictate which toppings to include in the lunchbox; the salad itself is quite tasty with all of them, some of them, or even with none.

Ingredients per serving:
¼–½ cup organic bananas, peeled and sliced or diced
¼–½ cup organic apples, washed, cored, and diced with the peel on
¼–½ cup fresh or frozen organic sliced strawberries (about ¼ cup per serving)
¼ cup organic vanilla yogurt; either regular or Greek-style will work nicely
2 tablespoons organic shredded or flaked coconut
2 tablespoons diced walnuts

Directions:
1) Combine the bananas, apples, and strawberries together in a medium bowl; the strawberries will help keep the other fruit from browning, and also give the salad a pleasant, rosy color.
2) Place the fruit in a sealable lunch bowl and add smaller containers of the desired toppings for our kiddo to sprinkle on before eating. Include a frozen gel pack, and remember to include a spoon, and possibly a fork, too!

Tip: Pick a variety of apple that tastes good when eaten out of hand, as opposed to a baking or cooking apple.

Strawberry Spinach Salad

Spinach and strawberries are two produce items you should place high on the organic list. Strawberries in particular tend to absorb pesticides, so that even if you wash them first you'll still be getting more than you bargained for when you eat them. Fortunately, both of these nutritious and delicious edibles are increasingly available organically grown. The tangy sweet dressing and mild cheese make this salad appealing to even the youngest kiddos. Substitute for or supplement the strawberries with orange sections or pineapple bits if you wish.

Ingredients per serving:
1 handful organic baby spinach leaves, well rinsed and patted dry
2–3 organic strawberries, rinsed, hulled, and sliced
2 tablespoons diced or shredded organic Swiss or mozzarella cheese
2 tablespoons slivered organic almonds, optional
½ cup Lemon Salad Dressing (p. 78)

Directions:
1) Place the spinach into the desired lunch container. Top with the strawberries and cheese, and the almonds, if using.
2) Pour the dressing into a small container to send with the salad; make sure it has a leakproof lid. Although the salad can be dressed prior to sending off to school, prolonged exposure to the liquid will tend to shrink the spinach and cause the strawberries to leak some of their moisture. It will still taste fine, but the texture will suffer a bit. Don't forget to add in a fork, or the salad may end up as finger food!

Lemon Salad Dressing

The poppy seeds add flavor and crunch to this dressing. However, if you prefer not to use them the dressing will be fine without. This also makes an excellent dressing for a fresh fruit salad.

Ingredients:
2 tablespoons organic lemon juice
1 tablespoon pure maple syrup, locally produced honey, or organic agave nectar
¼ teaspoon sea salt
⅛ teaspoon organic onion powder
1 teaspoon organic poppy seeds, optional
4 tablespoons organic olive oil

Directions:
1) Whisk together the lemon juice, maple syrup or other sweetener, salt, onion powder, and poppy seeds. Then, whisk in the olive oil until the dressing is slightly thickened.
2) Use at once or stir well before pouring. Leftovers may be stored, covered, in the refrigerator for up to 2 weeks.

Under the Sea Salad

Here is another easy-to-assemble main dish salad. Dressing for the vegetables is optional; your child may prefer them plain. The little fish add flavor and crunch as they swim through a reef of vegetables and on over the tuna fish salad.

Makes 2 servings.

Ingredients:
Tuna Salad Sandwich Filling (p. 52)
½ cup organic cherry or grape tomatoes
½ cup organic cucumber slices
¼ cup shredded organic carrot
½ cup little fish-shaped crackers (I have found these made with organic flour)
¼ cup organic salad dressing of choice, optional

Directions:
1) Place a mound of half the tuna salad in the middle of a serving dish. Add a ring of tomatoes, cut in half if you wish, and cucumber slices, around the tuna salad. Shred a bit of carrot over the top. Repeat with a second serving dish, or refrigerate the remaining ingredients for the next day.
2) Send to school with a frozen gel pack to keep it safe. Send the dressing, if your child likes it, and the little fish crackers in separate containers.
3) When it's time to eat, add the dressing to the veggies, sprinkle with little swimming cracker fish, and enjoy!

Kid-Sized Cobb Salad

Traditional Cobb salad features rows of various proteins and vegetables striped next to each other. The salad gets its name from Bob Cobb, who ran the Brown Derby restaurant in Hollywood, California, back in the 1920s and 1930s. I've eliminated some of the original ingredients, such as bacon, watercress, and Roquefort cheese, and substituted more organic and kid-friendly foods, including green peas and a bit of shredded or diced organic cheese, such as cheddar, Swiss, or provolone. You can add a sprinkling of chopped organic chives if your child enjoys such things. Dress as you wish, although I think a nice ranch-type dressing fits perfectly.

Ingredients:
Finely chopped organic lettuce
Diced organic tomato
Diced organic avocado, sprinkled lightly with lemon or lime juice to prevent browning
Fresh or frozen organic peas
Diced cooked organic chicken breast or turkey breast
Diced organic cheese
Chopped organic chives, optional
Organic ranch or other favorite dressing

Directions:
1) Prepare the salad directly in the serving dish your kiddo will be bringing to school. You can either stripe the various diced ingredients side by side, or layer them one on top of the other. I would suggest starting with the lettuce, but aside from that I don't think the order really matters; I just like to contrast the colors and flavors between the layers.
2) Cover the salad tightly and send to school with the dressing in a small separate container. Don't forget a fork to eat it with, and a frozen gel pack to keep it cool.

Hot or Cold

Tasty and Nutritious Entrees for the School Lunch Bunch

Safe Travels for Hot Lunches

The biggest challenge to sending your child to school with a nice hot lunch is how to keep it at a safe temperature until lunchtime. We were fortunate at my most recent school of employment to have two microwaves available for the kids to heat up their lunches. If your school offers this option, simply send the entrées cold, chilled with a reusable gel pack, in a well-insulated lunchbox. If your child does not have access to a microwave, you must decide whether to send the lunches chilled, just to be on the safe side, or to try to utilize a thermal container to keep casseroles or soups appealingly warm until it's time to eat them. The Safety.com website provides information on how to go about choosing and using a safe and appropriate thermal container (safety.com/blog/how-to-select-and-safely-use-a-thermos).

In general, look for containers that are BPA-free, phthalate-free (or within legal standards), and lead-free (or within legal standards). Follow the directions that come with the container you choose. In order to maintain a safe heat of approximately 160° F or above, start with hot (not warm) food that has adequate liquid in it. Don't save and try to reuse any uneaten food that might return home at the end of the day.

Fortunately, most of these entrées taste A-OK either hot or chilled, so simply decide what's best for your child's individual situation.

Kid-Friendly Baked Beans	85	Italian Mini Meatballs	101
Quick & Easy Chili	86	Buttery Tomato Pasta Rounds	103
Old-Fashioned Beef Stew	87	Crispy Oven-Fried Drumsticks	104
Shepherd's Pie As-You-Like-It	89	Three Buddies Dip	105
Beet Loaf Cupcakes	91	Chicken Nibbles	107
Meatloaf Cupcakes	93	Chicken-Fried Tofu	109
Creamy Whipped Potatoes	94	Sweet Potato Fritters	111
Fresh Italian Tomato Sauce	95	Honey Mustard Sauce	112
Pink Whipped Potatoes	97	Teriyaki Tofu	113
Golden Glow Mac & Cheese	99	Super Smoothies	115
Cheesy Tomato Bow Ties	100	Sautéed Rice and Veggies	119

Kid-Friendly Baked Beans

Technically, these beans are not baked; they come from a can, just like many of their fully prepared counterparts. However, the open-and-eat brands of beans frequently pack an overload of refined sugar and salt. Maple syrup, ketchup, mustard, and a splash of vinegar provide a slightly sweet and spicy sauce in this tasty organic alternative.

Makes 2–3 servings.

Ingredients:
15-ounce can organic great northern, pinto, or other light beans
2 tablespoons pure maple syrup
2 tablespoons organic ketchup
1 teaspoon organic prepared yellow mustard
1 tablespoon organic butter or organic coconut oil
1 teaspoon organic cider vinegar
Pinch organic ground cloves, optional
2–3 sliced organic hot dogs, optional

Directions:
1) Drain the canning liquid from the beans into a medium saucepan. Stir in the maple syrup, ketchup, mustard, butter or coconut oil, cider vinegar, and cloves. Heat the mixture over medium heat, stirring it smooth, until it begins to bubble.
2) Stir in the beans and allow everything to simmer over medium-low heat, uncovered, for about 20 minutes, stirring occasionally to prevent sticking. The sauce will thicken slightly and permeate the beans with flavor.
3) Because these are vegetarian, they should be fairly safe to transport hot in a good-quality thermos. If you choose to enhance your beans with some organic hot dog slices, I would suggest cooking in advance and sending them in a separate, chilled container to add in just before eating.

Quick & Easy Chili

. . . .

This mild and flavorful chili is easy to make with whatever protein you prefer. It's also a snap to prepare; 5 minutes to throw it together, another 20 to simmer and blend the flavors, and you're all set in under half an hour! Send it to school with some shredded cheddar for topping and a corn muffin to go with it. Organic corn tortilla chips for dipping in the chili are another option.

Makes 4–6 kid-sized servings.

Ingredients:
8 ounces organic or grass-fed ground beef or organic ground chicken or turkey
1 tablespoon organic vegetable oil, optional for browning poultry
15-ounce can organic red beans or kidney beans
16 ounces organic salsa
1 teaspoon organic cumin
½ teaspoon organic oregano
½ teaspoon organic garlic salt or ¼ teaspoon organic garlic powder
½ cup water

Directions:
1) Brown the ground meat in a large heavy skillet over medium-high heat, adding the oil only if necessary to prevent sticking. Add in all the remaining ingredients, stirring to blend well.
2) Reduce the heat to medium-low and allow the chili to simmer, uncovered, for 20 minutes, stirring occasionally. If the chili isn't thick enough for you at this time, allow it to simmer until it reaches the desired thickness.
3) Cool to room temperature before packing into leakproof containers for lunch. Send to school chilled with a frozen gel pack, or pour it boiling hot into a reliable thermos.

Old-Fashioned Beef Stew

I haven't included many beef recipes in *The Organic Lunchbox* for a few reasons. Organic beef is often hard to find and very expensive. Many of us are also decreasing or foregoing red meat in our diets. And, of course, anything with this much animal protein will require special handling to keep it safe until lunch; either a reliable thermos that will maintain a safe temperature (160° F) until lunchtime, or a reliable cold pack to keep it properly chilled. However, if your kid is a meat lover, this hearty and flavorful stew can provide a filling and nourishing lunch.

Makes 6 kid-sized servings.

Ingredients:

1 pound organic or humanely raised grass-fed stew beef

2 tablespoons organic olive oil

½ large or 1 small onion, peeled and chopped

1 stalk organic celery, rinsed and thinly sliced

1 clove organic garlic, peeled and diced

1 teaspoon sea salt

¼ teaspoon freshly ground organic black pepper

½ teaspoon organic paprika

2–3 teaspoons fresh snipped organic rosemary or 1 teaspoon dried rosemary

2–3 organic bay leaves

4 cups water

3 cups organic baby carrots

4½–5 cups organic red potatoes, scrubbed and cubed

¼ cup organic cornstarch or flour

Directions:

1) Cut the stew beef into fairly uniform cubes; I like them about 1 inch each. Heat the oil in a large, heavy saucepan over medium high. Add in the cubed beef and sauté, turning occasionally, until the beef is lightly browned.

2) Add in the onion, celery, and garlic and continue to sauté, stirring to prevent sticking, until the mixture is dark golden brown.

3) Add in all the seasonings and 4 cups of water. Bring to a boil, then lower the heat, cover, and boil gently for about 30 minutes, until the meat begins to tenderize.

4) Add the carrots in a layer on top and cook another 15 minutes. Stir the stew, then add the potatoes to the top, cover again, and cook an additional 15 minutes, or until the potatoes are just tender. Make sure your stew stays fairly juicy, with the water mostly covering the veggies.

5) Combine the cornstarch and ½–1 cup of water until smooth. Stir the mixture gently into the stew and cook until it is bubbly and thickened.

6) The stew can be served immediately, or cooled, uncovered, to room temperature. Store in the fridge in a covered container until you are ready to fill lunch thermoses; use the stew within 3–4 days. Heat to boiling just before filling thermoses. If lunch is more than 3 hours away, it might be better to ladle the cold stew into a microwavable bowl or dish and send along with a cold pack.

Shepherd's Pie As-You-Like-It

Shepherd's pie has long been the quintessential kid-friendly lunch. However, all shepherd's pie is not created equal. My vague memories of long-ago school lunches recall globs of flavorless ground beef mixed with canned corn of questionable origins, topped by instant mashed potatoes. I swore to never subject my own children to such an unfortunate variation of what could otherwise be a perfectly respectable meal, and I never did. This particular recipe is quite flexible and can be made using meat, poultry, or vegetarian ground meat substitute. Rather than topping the meat and vegetable base with the mashed potatoes, I keep them separate, to pack for lunches as you wish. Be sure to include a cold pack, especially if you make your shepherd's pie with ground beef or poultry.

Makes 6 kid-sized servings.

Ingredients:

1 pound organic or sustainably produced ground beef, turkey, chicken, or vegetarian substitute

½ cup diced onion

1 cup thinly sliced organic carrot

1 tablespoon organic vegetable oil, optional

½ teaspoon sea salt

¼ teaspoon organic black pepper

15-ounce can organic green beans, undrained

2 cups frozen loose-pack organic corn

2 tablespoons organic cornstarch

1 cup organic vegetable, beef, or chicken stock

Creamy Whipped Potatoes (p. 94)

Directions:

1) Combine the ground meat or substitute, diced onion, and sliced carrots in a heavy frying pan. Most meats contain enough fat so you don't need to add oil; however, if your meat is very lean, add up to 1 tablespoon to help prevent sticking. Cook over medium heat, stirring occasionally, until the meat begins to brown. Add in the salt and pepper, then cover and continue to cook another 5–10 minutes, until the carrots are tender.

2) Add in the green beans along with their canning liquid and the corn.

3) In a small bowl, stir together the cornstarch and stock until smooth, then add to the other ingredients.

4) Bring to a boil, stirring occasionally. Then, reduce the heat and simmer, covered, for about 10 minutes, until it has thickened and the flavors are well blended.

5) Allow to cool before packing for lunch. Place a serving of the meat and vegetable mixture and a serving of potato in the same or separate containers, whichever works best for you and your child. Make sure to send them well chilled, or heated to boiling (or very hot for the potatoes) before placing in a reliable thermos.

Tip: You may want a double the Creamy Whipped Potatoes recipe for this amount of Shepherd's Pie.

Beet Loaf Cupcakes

You don't need meat to make a delicious "meatloaf!" This recipe utilizes beets and black beans to make flavorful and colorful mini "beet loaves." Baking them in cupcake tins produces even portions and makes them easy and fun to eat. Frost Beet Loaf Cupcakes with your choice of traditional or beet-enhanced whipped potatoes for an unusual lunchbox treat. They also taste great unfrosted. Store in the refrigerator, or put them in a labeled resealable bag in the freezer for longer storage. I do not recommend frosting them if you are going to freeze them; mashed potatoes do not freeze well.

Makes 6–12 servings.

Ingredients:

12 paper baking cups
Organic nonstick cooking spray
2 tablespoons organic olive oil
⅓ cup diced onion
⅓ cup diced organic carrot
⅓ cup diced organic red bell pepper
1 clove organic garlic, minced finely
2 cups peeled, diced cooked organic beets

1 15-ounce can organic red or black beans
½ teaspoon sea salt
½ teaspoon organic oregano
1 teaspoon organic cumin, optional but good
½ cup organic rolled oats
2 large organic eggs, beaten

Directions:

1) Preheat the oven to 350° F. Place the baking cups in a muffin tin, and then spray them with nonstick cooking spray.
2) Heat the oil in a heavy skillet or frying pan over medium heat. Sauté the onions, carrots, and peppers in the hot oil just to soften them—you don't want to brown the veggies. Just before removing from the heat, stir in the garlic to heat through.
3) In a blender or food processor, blend together the beets and undrained beans until mostly smooth.
4) Add to the sautéed vegetables, along with the salt, oregano, cumin, rolled oats, and eggs.
5) Divide the mixture evenly among the prepared muffin cups. Bake for 45–50 minutes, until the mini beet loaves are firm on top when lightly touched.
6) Allow to cool slightly in the pan before frosting with Creamy Whipped Potatoes (p. 94) or Pink Whipped Potatoes (p. 97). The beet cakes can also be stored or served as is.

Tip: Using paper baking cups will enable you to remove the beet loaves from the muffin tins much more effectively.

Meatloaf Cupcakes

When I was a kid, I absolutely loved meatloaf. I still do! Not to mention, it is a great way to stretch your protein while adding in a few healthy and flavorful veggies; something we can all benefit from. In the spirit of food being fun, these mini loaves are formed into little cupcakes. Baking meatloaf in cupcake tins yields evenly portioned servings that can be eaten either as finger food or with a fork. They are tasty as is; even better topped with Creamy Whipped Potatoes (p. 94) or Pink Whipped Potatoes (p. 97).

Makes 6–12 servings.

Ingredients:
12 paper baking cups
1 pound organic or humanely raised grass-fed ground beef or organic ground turkey
2 organic eggs
¼ cup finely shredded organic carrot
¼ cup finely shredded organic zucchini
2–4 tablespoons finely minced organic onion
½ cup organic rolled oats
¼ cup organic ketchup
¾ teaspoon sea salt
⅛ teaspoon organic black pepper
½ teaspoon mixed Italian herbs, or other favorite organic herbs, optional

Directions:
1) Preheat the oven to 350° F. Line a muffin tin with paper baking cups.
2) Mix all the meatloaf ingredients together in a large bowl until they are totally combined.
3) Divide the mixture evenly between the muffin cups, smoothing the tops level.
4) Bake for 45–50 minutes, until the tops are lightly browned and feel firm to touch.
5) Remove from oven and allow to cool for about 10 minutes before adding potato frosting.
6) Allow the "cupcakes" to cool for about 30 minutes before refrigerating. Leave them right in the muffin tins, or remove to portable lunch containers once they have cooled. Make sure to add an ice pack when packing for lunch. These may be frozen, unfrosted, for longer storage.

Creamy Whipped Potatoes

This is a little softer and creamier than traditional mashed potatoes to facilitate easy spreading. Russet potatoes are a good choice due to their low starch content, allowing them to be whipped without turning into paste. A bit of cream cheese enriches the potatoes, making them even more "frosting" worthy, although they are also quite tasty accompanying a variety of dishes.

Makes 1½ cups; 3 servings or enough to frost 6 Meatloaf or Beet Loaf Cupcakes.

Ingredients:
2½ cups peeled, cubed organic russet potatoes
½ teaspoon sea salt, plus additional for seasoning
1 tablespoon organic butter
1 ounce organic cream cheese
¼ cup organic milk
Organic black pepper

Directions:
1) Place the potatoes in a medium saucepan with ½ teaspoon salt and enough water just to cover. Bring to a boil, then reduce heat and boil gently until they are fork tender, about 15–20 minutes.
2) Drain the cooked potatoes well, then add the butter, cream cheese, and milk and heat just to melt the butter.
3) Beat with a hand mixer until smooth and creamy.
4) Season to taste with pepper and additional salt, if desired.

Fresh Italian Tomato Sauce

This sauce is very versatile—use for pasta, pizza, and dipping! It's a good one to make while organic tomatoes are in season, and it can easily be frozen in serving-size containers. Try doubling or tripling the recipe if you want to freeze some for later use. It will also keep in the refrigerator, covered, for approximately 1 week.

Makes 1½–2 cups of sauce.

Ingredients:
2 pounds organic paste tomatoes, such as Roma
¼ cup chopped organic onion
1 large clove organic garlic, peeled and diced
1 tablespoon fresh snipped organic oregano leaves or 1 teaspoon dried
1 tablespoon fresh snipped organic Italian basil or 1 teaspoon dried
2 tablespoons organic olive oil
1 organic bay leaf
¼ teaspoon sea salt
3–4 grinds organic black pepper

Directions:
1) Dip the tomatoes in a large pan of boiling water for about 30 seconds to loosen the skins. Submerge in cold water until they are cool enough to handle. Slip the skins off and, using your thumb, push out the seeds, leaving the tomato flesh for the sauce. If the tomatoes are large, it may be easier to cut them in half prior to removing the seeds.
2) Place the onion and garlic in a blender or food processor and blend or process until mostly smooth. Add in the tomatoes, oregano, and basil, blending again until everything is nicely pureed.
3) Heat the olive oil in a large sauce pan over medium heat.
4) Pour in the pureed tomato mixture, adding in the bay leaf, salt, and pepper. Bring to a boil, then reduce the heat and simmer for about 30 minutes, until the sauce is somewhat thickened.
5) Remove from heat to use right away, or cool to room temperature before placing in lidded container(s) and refrigerating or freezing for future use.

Pink Whipped Potatoes

The lower starch content of the russet potatoes allows them to be beaten smooth and creamy without turning into a paste. The amount of milk specified along with the butter should turn your pink potatoes into a soft, creamy "frosting." Pureed beets add a surprising pink tint to this not-at-all sweet "frosting." They are also tasty when served as a traditional side dish.

Makes 1½ cups; 3 servings or enough to frost 6 Beet Loaf or Meatloaf Cupcakes.

Ingredients:
2½ cups peeled, cubed organic russet potatoes
½ teaspoon sea salt, plus additional for seasoning
1–2 tablespoons organic butter
¼ cup organic whole milk
2 tablespoons Garnet Beet Puree (p. 146)

Directions:
1) Place the potatoes in a medium saucepan with ½ teaspoon salt and enough water just to cover. Bring to a boil, then reduce heat and boil gently until they are fork tender, about 15–20 minutes.
2) Drain the cooked potatoes well, then add the butter and milk and heat just to melt the butter.
3) Beat with a hand mixer until smooth and creamy, integrating the beet puree near the end.
4) Taste for seasoning, adding a bit more salt if desired.
5) Use to frost meatloaf or beet loaf cupcakes, or serve as a fun side dish.

Golden Glow Mac & Cheese

Macaroni and cheese doesn't need artificial coloring to attain that pleasing golden color. The carrots add both color and nutritional value; great news if you have a kid or two with an aversion to vegetables. Including a bit of cream cheese makes the dish extra creamy and flavorful, with lots of cheesy sauce surrounding the cooked pasta.

Makes about 3 kid-sized servings.

Ingredients:

1 cup finely shredded organic carrot
½ cup water
1 cup organic elbow macaroni or other preferred pasta
2 tablespoons organic butter
2 tablespoons organic cornstarch or flour
¾ teaspoon seasoned salt
½ teaspoon dry mustard powder

1 cup organic milk
1 cup shredded organic cheddar cheese
2 ounces regular or low-fat organic cream
   cheese
Sea salt, as needed
Organic cheese crackers, squares or bunny
   shaped, optional

Directions:

1) Combine the shredded carrot and water in a small saucepan. Cover and bring to a boil. Boil for about 5 minutes over medium heat, until the shredded carrots are just tender. Do not drain them. Allow them to cool for a few minutes before pureeing them and their cooking water until the mixture is smooth.
2) While that cools, start cooking the macaroni according to the directions on the box.
3) While the macaroni is cooking, melt the butter over low heat in a medium saucepan. Stir in the cornstarch or flour, seasoned salt, and dry mustard. Stir and cook for 1–2 minutes.
4) Using a whisk, add the milk and the pureed carrot to the pan all at once and cook over medium heat, whisking to keep it smooth, until it boils and thickens.
5) Whisk in the cheddar cheese and cream cheese until the sauce is again smooth.
6) Carefully pour the macaroni and cooking water into a sieve that has been placed over the sink and drain the macaroni well.
7) Stir the hot macaroni into the hot cheese sauce, stirring gently to mix well.
8) This can be eaten as is, or pour it into a casserole dish, sprinkle cheese crackers over the top, and bake in a 350° F oven for about 20 minutes, until it is nice and bubbly.
9) When packing for school lunch, fill a preheated thermos with the hot mac and cheese or send it chilled in an insulated serving bowl for heating at school. Add a little container of crackers to sprinkle on when eating.

Tips: Substitute a teaspoon of prepared organic yellow mustard for the mustard powder if you prefer (add it when you add the liquids).
The seasoned salt adds nice flavor, but usually is not organic. If you wish, use ¼ teaspoon each organic paprika, onion powder, and pepper in place of the seasoned salt.

Cheesy Tomato Bow Ties

Bow tie pasta makes this tasty dish extra fun, although other shapes can easily be used. Try substituting organic cottage cheese if you can't find organic ricotta. Add mini meatballs or not, as you wish.

Makes 2 good sized "little kid" serving portions.

Ingredients:
1 cup uncooked organic bow tie pasta
¼ cup organic ricotta cheese
½ cup Fresh Italian Tomato Sauce (p. 95) or smooth marinara sauce of your choice
¼ cup organic shredded mozzarella cheese

Directions:
1) Cook the pasta according to the package directions until it is just tender.
2) Drain well and return to the cooking pan over low heat. Stir in the ricotta, allowing it to melt and blend with the pasta. Add the tomato sauce and then the mozzarella, stirring quickly to just blend well. (The mozzarella will turn stringy as it melts.)
3) Fill a reliable thermos with the hot pasta. If you add meatballs, you may wish to send them chilled in a separate container to add to the hot pasta just before eating.

Italian Mini Meatballs

These tiny meatballs are kid-sized, kind of like you might get out of a can of pasta only better. Add a few to Buttery Tomato Pasta Rounds (p. 103) if you'd like a meat-enhanced version, or simply send them along in their own little container as the protein component to any variety of lunches. Make sure to keep them properly chilled so the meat stays at a safe temperature.

Makes 6–8 servings.

Ingredients:
1 pound organic or humanely raised grass-fed ground beef or ground organic turkey
1 organic egg
½ teaspoon sea salt
⅛ teaspoon organic black pepper
2 tablespoons grated organic Parmesan cheese
2 tablespoons finely chopped fresh organic parsley or 2 teaspoons dried
½ teaspoon organic garlic powder or 1 clove organic garlic, peeled and minced
2 tablespoons cold water
1 tablespoon organic olive oil

Directions:
1) Combine all ingredients except the olive oil in a large bowl, being sure to thoroughly mix everything together.
2) Form the mixture evenly into 32 small meatballs.
3) Heat the oil in a heavy skillet over medium-low heat.
4) Place the meatballs in the skillet with the oil and cook for about 5 minutes, shaking occasionally to prevent the meatballs from sticking.
5) Carefully turn all the mini meatballs browned side up, cover the pan, and cook for another 5 minutes, until the meatballs have lost all their pinkness and are done through.
6) Cool quickly to room temperature and refrigerate until ready to use. Freeze for longer storage; use within 1 month.

Tip: One easy way to guesstimate meatball size is to divide the mixture into fourths, and then each fourth into four again. Finally, divide each piece of meatball mix into two, giving you a grand total of 32 mini meatballs. If you have the patience to go even smaller, make the final division into thirds instead of halves, giving you 48 even tinier meatballs.

Buttery Tomato Pasta Rounds

If you're familiar with the pasta rounds that come out of a can, you know that they are blander and sweeter than homemade pasta sauce. Unfortunately, this usually equates to added sugar and fillers. In this recipe, sweet potato lightens up the sauce, adding a nutritional boost along with sweetness. There is very little salt in this sauce; adding a slight sprinkle of sea salt may enhance that more familiar taste some kids are accustomed to. Serve the Buttery Tomato Pasta Rounds as is, or add in a few mini meatballs if you prefer. If you are unable to locate organic pasta rounds in your local supermarket, other shapes can easily be substituted.

Makes 2 servings.

Ingredients:
1 cup organic pasta rounds
½ cup Golden Sweet Potato Puree (p. 143)
½ cup Fresh Italian Tomato Sauce (p. 95)
1 tablespoon organic butter
2 tablespoons grated organic Parmesan cheese

Directions:
1) Cook the pasta rounds according to the package directions until they are just tender.
2) While the pasta is cooking, combine the sweet potato puree, tomato sauce, and butter in a small pan, simmering until the butter melts.
3) Drain the cooked pasta well and return to cooking pan. Stir in the sauce. Sprinkle the grated cheese evenly over the top and gently stir it in; if it is added in a pile, it may have a tendency to clump together.
4) If you choose to add meatballs, make sure they are heated thoroughly before placing everything in a reliable thermos, or keep them separate with an iced gel pack and combine just before eating.

Crispy Oven-Fried Drumsticks

Fried chicken is another time-tested kid favorite. This flavorful version contains much less fat than deep-fried chicken, and baking allows more even browning than pan frying does. Send with your child's favorite healthy sides for a hearty and delicious school lunch.

Makes 4–6 servings.

Ingredients:
2 cups organic crispy rice or corn cereal, finely crushed
½ teaspoon sea salt
½ teaspoon organic paprika
1 teaspoon organic dried parsley flakes
½ teaspoon organic dried thyme
¼ teaspoon fresh ground organic pepper
2 pounds organic chicken drumsticks, about 6–8, or 3 organic chicken legs, cut at the joint into thighs and drumsticks
2 tablespoons organic butter
2 tablespoons organic olive oil

Directions:
1) Place the crushed cereal in a bowl and combine with the salt, paprika, parsley, thyme, and pepper, mixing well.
2) Adjust your oven rack to the middle position, and preheat the oven to 375° F.
3) Place the butter and olive oil in a 9-by-13-inch baking pan and place in the heating oven to melt the butter; it should only take a couple of minutes.
4) Remove the pan from the oven and swirl the butter and oil together.
5) Coat each chicken piece on all sides with the butter and oil mixture, and then coat generously with the seasoned crumbs.
6) Place the pieces of chicken, skin side up, back in the pan, ensuring that the pieces are not touching.
7) Bake for approximately 1 hour, until the chicken is golden brown, crispy, and the juices run clear when pierced with a fork.
8) Chill well before sending for lunch accompanied by an iced gel pack.

Tip: The cereal can be easily crushed by placing it in a plastic food storage bag and rolling with a rolling pin, or you can simply process it for a few seconds in a food processor or blender. In either case, you should end up with about ¾ cup of cereal crumbs.

Three Buddies Dip

This tasty dip is easy peasy to concoct and makes a great condiment as either a dip or sandwich spread. Vary the amounts of ketchup, mayonnaise, and yogurt to make as much or as little as you desire, simply double or quadruple them.

Ingredients:
2 tablespoons organic ketchup
2 tablespoons organic mayonnaise
2 tablespoons plain organic Greek-style yogurt
A dash of hot sauce, optional

Directions:
1) Mix all the ingredients together. Store, covered, in the refrigerator to prevent discoloration and keep fresh.
2) Send to school in individual serving containers, making sure to keep them cool along the way.

Chicken Nibbles

We're all familiar with those fast food pieces of bite-sized chicken. What you may not be so familiar with is the long list of ingredients that frequently accompanies them. While there have been efforts in recent years to decrease the use of mechanically separated chicken in these products, I still prefer making my own using fresh organic chicken breast meat.

Makes about 3 kid-sized servings.

Ingredients:
8 ounces skinless, boneless organic chicken breast meat
½ cup organic or BST-free buttermilk or ½ cup organic milk plus 1 teaspoon organic lemon juice
A few drops of hot sauce, optional
¼ cup organic all-purpose flour
2 tablespoons organic cornstarch
2 tablespoons organic yellow cornmeal
½ teaspoon sea salt
¼ teaspoon organic paprika
¼ teaspoon organic garlic powder
⅛ teaspoon fresh ground organic black pepper
1 teaspoon organic parsley flakes
½ cup organic vegetable oil

Directions:
1) Cut the chicken into bite-size pieces. Combine in a small bowl with the buttermilk and the pepper sauce, if using, turning to cover well. Allow to sit for at least 10 minutes and up to 30 minutes.
2) Meanwhile, combine the flour, cornstarch, cornmeal, salt, paprika, garlic powder, black pepper, and parsley flakes in another small bowl and mix together well.
3) Heat the oil in a medium-size heavy skillet over medium heat.
4) Dip the chicken pieces into the flour mixture to coat well. Fry a few at a time in the hot oil until nicely browned on both sides. Try cutting into one piece to test for doneness; it should be still juicy in appearance but with no pink left, which would indicate undercooking. Drain on paper towels or parchment paper until cooled to room temperature.
5) Place in serving-size containers and refrigerate until ready to send for lunch. Include an iced gel pack and your child's desired dipping sauce; organic ketchup, Three Buddies Dip (p. 106), or Honey Mustard Sauce (p. 112) are all good options.

Chicken-Fried Tofu

I first created a recipe for Chicken-Fried Tofu for one of my teacher friends who is a vegetarian. I've added a few touches over the years to make it even tastier for kids and adults alike. A prolonged soaking time in the flavorful broth is the secret to making these vegetarian/vegan nuggets taste like little bites of chicken.

Makes 4–6 kid-sized servings.

Ingredients:

1 pound extra firm organic tofu
2 cups organic no-chicken broth (I prefer Imagine brand)
Organic flour for dipping, about ½ cup
3 tablespoons organic butter or vegan margarine
3 tablespoons organic vegetable oil
Crispy coating:
2 cups organic rice, corn, or wheat crispy cereal, finely crushed

½ teaspoon sea salt
Few grinds organic black pepper
½ teaspoon organic paprika
½ teaspoon organic garlic powder
2 teaspoons organic parsley flakes
½ teaspoon poultry seasoning or substitute any combination of organic thyme, rosemary, or sage to equal ½ teaspoon
Organic nonstick cooking spray or oil

Directions:

1) Cut the tofu into small cubes. Place the cubes into a container with the broth and refrigerate for at least two days or up to four days for the best flavor.
2) When you're ready to prepare it, preheat the oven to 400°F.
3) Combine the finely crushed cereal in a small bowl with the salt, pepper, paprika, garlic powder, parsley, and other herbs of choice.
4) Place the flour in another small bowl.
5) Drain the tofu well.
6) Melt together the butter or margarine and the vegetable oil in a small saucepan, then remove from the heat.
7) Dip the tofu pieces first in the flour, then in the butter/oil mixture, and finally into the seasoned crumbs. Place them on a parchment paper–lined baking sheet that has been sprayed with organic nonstick cooking spray or brushed with organic oil.
8) Bake for 35–40 minutes, until the little pieces are nicely browned and have shrunk slightly. At this point the coating will be crispy and the outer part of the tofu will have lost enough moisture to be slightly chewy while the inside remains tender.
9) Serve just the way they are, or side them with Honey Mustard Sauce (p. 112) or Three Buddies Dip (p. 105). Be sure to refrigerate prior to serving. Sending them with a chilled gel pack is a good idea, especially on a hot day, although these are not as perishable as meat-based nibbles would be. They may also be frozen for up to 1 month.

Sweet Potato Fritters

Sweet Potato Fritters are little nuggets of golden goodness that make a great accompaniment to Chicken Nibbles (p. 107), Chicken-Fried Tofu (p. 109), or even the Maple Sausage Patties (p. 13) or Slightly Spicy Sausage Patties (p. 12) found in the Breakfast for Lunch section. They're hearty enough to stand by themselves as a vegetarian entrée, if you prefer. Try siding them with Honey Mustard Sauce (p. 112) for a tasty condiment.

Makes 3–4 servings.

Ingredients:
2 cups precooked organic shredded sweet potato
1 tablespoon organic cornstarch or flour
1 organic egg, beaten
¼ teaspoon sea salt
⅛ teaspoon grated organic nutmeg
Organic oil for frying

Directions:
1) Shred the cooled sweet potato and combine with everything except the oil.
2) Form the mixture into about a dozen evenly rounded patties.
3) Heat the oil in a heavy frying pan or skillet over medium-high heat.
4) Fry the patties in hot oil until they are golden on both sides and cooked throughout.
5) Cool before packing and refrigerating for lunch. Plan on 3–4 patties per child; a few more if they are to be the main entrée.

Tip: Leftover baked sweet potato works well for this recipe, or you could bake or microwave one until it is just tender; you don't want it overcooked or mushy. Boiled sweet potatoes do not work well for this recipe because of their higher water content.

Honey Mustard Sauce

This goes especially nicely with Sweet Potato Fritters (p. 111), Chicken-Fried Tofu (p. 109), or Chicken Nibbles (p. 107). It also makes a tasty sandwich spread for turkey, chicken, or ham.

Ingredients:
6 tablespoon locally produced honey
2 tablespoons organic yellow mustard
1 tablespoon plain organic Greek yogurt

Directions:
1) Cream together the honey and mustard; the mixture will be quite runny. Once it is smooth, stir in the yogurt.
2) Store in the fridge, and send to school in leakproof containers.

Teriyaki Tofu

Because of its neutral flavor, tofu is a perfect candidate for marinating in flavorful sauces. The Asian-inspired sauce in this recipe doubles as a marinade and then a glaze for the tofu cubes. They can be enjoyed by themselves with any side of choice. Serving them over Sautéed Rice and Veggies (p. 119) will provide a tasty complete meal that's easy to tuck into a lunchbox. Because the protein is plant based, serving at room temperature is less of a concern than when meat is involved. However, when storing any longer than a few hours, refrigeration is the prudent choice.

Makes 4–6 kid-sized servings.

Ingredients:
1 pound extra firm organic tofu
Marinade:
2 tablespoons packed organic brown sugar
2 tablespoons organic soy sauce or tamari
2 tablespoons organic vegetable oil
1 teaspoon finely diced or grated organic ginger root
1 teaspoon finely diced or grated organic garlic
2 teaspoons organic lime juice
Oil for frying

Directions:
1) Cut the tofu into cubes or rectangles. I do this by cutting it into 8 even slices, removing it from the liquid it is packed in, and then cutting each slice in half length-wise and thirds crosswise.
2) Combine all the marinade ingredients in a small to medium flat-bottomed bowl or other container. Add the tofu cubes, stirring gently to coat evenly without breaking up the tofu. Refrigerate and allow to marinate at least 4 hours; overnight is better. Turn the cubes every once in a while, so that they soak up the flavor evenly.
3) Drain the cubes well, reserving the marinade.
4) Heat a small amount of oil, just enough to cover the bottom and prevent the tofu from sticking, in a heavy skillet or frying pan.
5) Sauté the cubes over high heat, turning gently once or twice, until they have browned nicely. During the last minute or so of cooking, add in the marinade, again stirring gently to evaporate the liquid and glaze the tofu cubes.
6) Serve hot or at room temperature over Sautéed Rice and Veggies. Because tofu does not contain animal protein, it isn't as perishable as meat; however, a cold pack is always a good idea, especially if it's a very hot day. Teriyaki Tofu should also be stored in the refrigerator until ready to send to school.

Super Smoothies

If your kiddo prefers something a little lighter for lunch, smoothies may be the answer for you. They are also a great way to integrate more fruits into the diet—important sources of vital nutrients. Not to mention, they are an easy fix on a busy morning; any of these smoothies can be concocted in less than 5 minutes. If you and/or your kid happen to be dairy-free, substitute your favorite non-dairy yogurt in place of the Greek-style yogurt listed in some of the recipes; simply keep in mind whether there are any allergy precautions at your child's school when substituting plant-based products for dairy. Send in a well-insulated thermos that reliably keeps liquids cold.

Blueberry Bounty Smoothie

Blueberries enhance the antioxidant value of this mellow smoothie. Frozen berries blend in particularly well, although fresh blueberries also work fine. Due to the seeds and skin of the blueberries, this smoothie will have a bit more texture than its peach counterpart. The tiny hint of spice adds a nice touch, making it taste almost like blueberry pie. Grape juice deepens the blueish-purple color, while apple juice gives it a paler tinge. Either way it is delicious!

Makes 1 serving.

Ingredients:
½ cup fresh or frozen organic blueberries
½ cup organic apple or grape juice
¼ cup plain organic Greek-style yogurt
2 tablespoons quick-cooking organic rolled oats
Dash of organic cinnamon and/or nutmeg, optional

Directions:
1) Whirl all the ingredients together in a blender until smooth.

Double Berry Smoothie

This is the only smoothie I have suggested adding a tiny bit of extra sweetening to, because the berries may be a bit more tart than the other fruits used. However, it may also taste perfectly fine without any honey or syrup, depending on the sweetness of the berries, how much the milk mellows the flavor, and personal taste. Remember, kids usually develop a taste for sweets based on what they are exposed to. However, if she/he already prefers things a bit sweet, that little extra boost may make the difference between a smoothie consumed or a smoothie neglected.

Makes 1 serving.

Ingredients:
½ cup washed and hulled fresh or frozen organic strawberries
½ cup fresh or frozen organic red raspberries
¼ cup plain organic Greek-style yogurt
¼ cup organic dairy or rice milk
1–2 teaspoons locally sourced honey, pure maple syrup, or organic agave nectar, optional

Directions:
1) Combine all the ingredients in a blender, whirling until well blended.

Tip: The seeds in the berries, especially the raspberries, will not blend smooth. Generally, they will sink to the bottom of the serving container, making that last sip or two not quite as silky as the rest. Many kids won't mind this. However, if you want to make the smoothie a little smoother, blend the raspberries separately first, and then push them through a fine sieve to remove most of the seeds before adding back into the rest of the ingredients.

Just Peachy Smoothie

Rolled oats add extra fiber and nutrition to this classically flavored smoothie. Beet puree adds a tiny nutritional boost, but also colors the smoothie that classic peach color we all love so much; keep a supply of beet puree "ice cubes" in the freezer to make this easy as can be. It really doesn't add any flavor of its own to the smoothie. A drop or two of vanilla extract and/or almond extract will enhance the peachiness even more.

Makes 1 serving.

Ingredients:
½ cup juice-packed organic peaches, drained, or ½ cup fresh or frozen, thawed organic peaches
½ cup organic orange juice
¼ cup plain organic Greek-style yogurt
2 tablespoons quick-cooking organic rolled oats
1–2 teaspoons organic beet puree, optional
⅛ teaspoon organic vanilla extract and/or almond extract, optional

Directions:
1) Whirl all the ingredients in a blender until smooth; the rolled oats will add a bit of texture even after blending.

Nutty Banana Smoothie

Adding a bit of soy or nut butter gives this smoothie an extra protein boost, especially important if your child is a bit of a finicky eater. Just remember to check your school's dietary guidelines regarding tree nuts. Keep it chilled and spill-proof on the way to school.

Makes 1 serving.

Ingredients:
½ large or 1 small banana, peeled
1 tablespoon organic soy butter or nut butter, such as cashew or pecan
¼ cup plain organic Greek-style yogurt
½ cup organic orange or pineapple juice

Directions:
1) Break the banana into pieces and place in the blender with the soy or nut butter and the yogurt. Blend until thick and smooth.
2) Add the juice and blend again until smooth and drinkable.

Sunshine Smoothie

This sunny orange shake is a nutritional powerhouse; packed full of fruit, with an extra boost from sweet potato! This is a nice way to use up a bit of leftover cooked sweet potato, as long as it doesn't have added butter or seasonings and isn't too watery. Substituting 2 tablespoons of Golden Sweet Potato Puree (p. 143) is another option. You can also substitute peaches for the mango, if you wish. The pineapple juice helps prevent the smoothie from discoloring.

Makes 1 serving.

Ingredients:
½ medium banana, peeled
½ cup organic sliced or diced, peeled mango
½ cup organic pineapple juice
¼ cup diced organic sweet potato or 2 tablespoons pureed

Directions:
1) Combine all ingredients in a blender and whirl until smooth and thick.
2) As with all the smoothies, it is best when enjoyed quickly or placed in your favorite insulated beverage container for lunchtime refreshment.

Sautéed Rice and Veggies

Use your preference of white or brown rice; since it will have been cooked in advance, it won't affect the cooking time of this recipe. Although I think bright green peas are a great kid-friendly add-in vegetable, diced, lightly cooked green beans, broccoli, or even asparagus may be substituted, if you wish.

Makes 4 kid-sized servings.

Ingredients:
2 tablespoons organic olive or vegetable oil
1½ cups cooked organic rice
1 cup organic green peas (frozen loose pack)
2 tablespoons diced organic green onion or chives
1 tablespoon minced organic parsley
Sea salt and organic black pepper, to taste

Directions:
1) Heat the oil in a heavy skillet over medium-high heat.
2) Add in the rice, peas, green onions or chives, and the parsley, stirring occasionally, until the mixture is hot and the peas are cooked. This won't take long, as you want them to retain their nice bright color and nutritional value.
3) Season to taste with salt and pepper, then serve immediately or cool slightly before dividing into individual containers and topping with the Teriyaki Tofu (p. 113).
4) Refrigerate for safe storage. Although it should be fine to send to school as is, please add a gel pack if the weather is hot or the wait to lunch is longer than 3 hours.

Tip: This also makes a nice accompaniment to any of the other chicken or tofu dishes listed.

Veggies, Munchies, Dips & Breads

Variety Is the Spice of Life

Most children love easy-to-eat finger foods. Vegetables, plain or with dip, fit perfectly into this category. Serve up a nice variety of them for easy organic eating. Munchies, such as home-made veggie chips and crackers, can be fun and nourishing complements to sandwiches and soups, adding color and variety to your child's lunch choices. Just remember, organic produce, while pesticide free, can still harbor harmful bacteria. Be sure to wash well before packing for lunch.

Sending mini sliders in place of full-sized sandwiches is especially nice for younger children, although older kids can always bring two or three to fit growing appetites! You might wish to consider some of the more unusual breads, such as Rainbow Swirl (p. 147) or Soft Pretzels (p. 152) for a family baking adventure on a day when you all have a little extra time together.

Crispy Kale Chips

The classroom just down the hall from ours was famous for turning their fall kale harvest into these tasty kale chips. They are truly a snap to make; one of the easiest snacks you'll ever enjoy! You will need to watch them fairly closely—the trick is for the slightly thicker centers near the stems to crisp before the curly edges begin to brown and burn. Kale chips are more delicate than other veggie chips, and they crumble quite easily.

Makes 2–3 servings.

Ingredients:
Fresh organic kale (I prefer the curly leaved for this recipe, but any type can be used)
Organic olive oil
Sea salt

Directions:
1) Rinse the kale well and pat dry. Tear each leaf into chip-sized pieces, using only the tender outer portions and discarding the tough stems (or repurposing them for soup).
2) Ensure your oven rack is placed in the middle position, then preheat the oven to 350° F.
3) Place a wire rack over a large baking sheet. Toss the kale with a little olive oil, coating well. Use about 2 tablespoons of oil per 3–4 cups of loosely packed kale.
4) Place the kale on top of the rack. Sprinkle with a bit of sea salt, if you wish.
5) Bake for 15–20 minutes. The kale will turn dry and crispy; tossing the kale lightly every 5 minutes near the end of baking will help prevent burning.
6) Store in airtight containers to retain freshness. Plan to use within 2 weeks.

Tip: Crispy Kale Chips are delicious plain, or as an accompaniment to sandwiches or creamy soups.

Beet Chips

I have found the trick to making crispy but not burned beet chips is to cut them on the second thinnest setting of my food processor. The finest setting, which cuts them paper thin, doesn't allow enough beet to make a decent sized chip, and it also makes it virtually impossible to crisp the chips without burning them. The second setting, on the other hand, will give you nice crisp beet chips that also retain much of their vibrant color. These may also be hand-cut using a mandoline or sharp knife, although it may be a bit challenging to produce uniformly sized thin chips.

Makes 2–3 servings.

Ingredients:
3 tablespoons organic coconut oil
Organic beets, scrubbed and peeled, enough to yield 3–4 cups finely sliced beets
Sea salt, optional

Directions:
1) Preheat your oven to 350° F. Place the coconut oil on a large rimmed baking sheet and warm in the oven long enough to melt the oil.
2) Remove the baking sheet from the oven and swirl the melted oil evenly over the surface of the baking sheet.
3) Once the oil is cool enough to handle without burning yourself, sprinkle the beet slices onto the sheet, tossing them lightly with your fingers to coat with the oil and disburse them evenly over the baking sheet.
4) Put the pan on a rack positioned in the middle of the oven. Bake for approximately 20 minutes.
5) Remove the pan from the oven and redistribute the chips using a broad fork or deep-fat frying tool. Return to the oven, checking and stirring every 5 minutes or so, until the beet chips are crispy. The whole process will take approximately 30 minutes. Lightly browned chips will have a slightly sweeter flavor from the caramelization process, while the redder chips add color and a subtle taste appeal of their own.
6) Once done to your liking, remove the pan from the oven and allow the chips to cool thoroughly on the baking sheet. Add a sprinkle of sea salt, if you wish.
7) Store in an airtight container to retain crispness. Plan to use within 1 month.

Sweet Potato Chips

Sweet potatoes are packed with nutrients. How convenient that they also transform into a tasty chip! These sweet potato chips are so crispy and delicious that I don't even add salt. However, a little sprinkle can enhance the flavor, if you prefer. Smaller sweet potatoes work better for this, or larger ones can be halved lengthwise. There is no deep frying involved, they are simply roasted with a little coconut oil right in the oven.

Makes 2–3 servings.

Ingredients:
3–4 cups very thinly sliced sweet potatoes
3 tablespoons organic coconut oil
Sea salt, optional

Directions:
1) Preheat the oven to 350° F.
2) While the oven is preheating, place the coconut oil on a large rimmed baking sheet and pop it into the oven to melt the oil. Remove from the oven and swirl the melted oil to evenly coat the entire surface.
3) Once the pan is cool enough to touch, add the thinly sliced sweet potatoes, mixing well to coat each with some of the oil. Spread them out evenly and bake for approximately 20 minutes. Stir the slices to redistribute—this will help them brown and crisp evenly.
4) Continue baking, stirring the chips every 5 minutes, until they are golden and crispy; about 30 minutes total baking time. If they're not quite crisp, but you don't want them much darker, simply turn off the oven and leave the pan inside with the door shut for a few minutes (but not too long or they could overbrown even with the oven off).
5) Sprinkle them with a bit of sea salt, if you wish, while they're still warm.
6) Store in an airtight bag or container to retain freshness; plan to use within 1 month.

Tip: There is no need to peel the sweet potatoes for this recipe, although you will want to scrub them well and remove any blemishes. Slice them very thin using either a food processor, mandoline, or sharp knife. I find setting my processor blade to the second thinnest setting enables the chips to crisp nicely but still have some substance.

Parsnip Chips

Parsnips, a cousin of the more familiar carrots, give a new twist to snacking chips. Although they resemble potato chips, the taste of Parsnip Chips is unique—slightly sweet with a hint of spice, even though no spice is included in their preparation. There is no need to peel them, simply slice very thin and roast in a bit of coconut oil. Because of the parsnip's lighter color, these chips roast at a slightly higher oven temperature than the others in this book.

Makes 2 servings.

Ingredients:
Organic whole parsnips, scrubbed well
Organic coconut oil
Sea salt, optional

Directions:
1) Preheat the oven to 375° F.
2) Slice the whole parsnips into very thin slices using a food processor, kitchen mandoline, or grater—being careful not to slice a finger in the process! I prefer my food processor set to the second thinnest setting; paper thin is a little too thin to form a proper chip.
3) Melt about 1 tablespoon of coconut oil for every 1½ cups of sliced parsnips directly on a rimmed baking sheet that's large enough to hold the parsnip chips in a single layer.
4) Toss the slices gently with the melted oil to coat them thoroughly.
5) Bake for a total of 25–30 minutes, stirring the chips every 5–10 minutes to prevent them from sticking to one another and to facilitate even browning. You'll know they're done when they are golden around the edges and the white part of the slice appears opaque rather than shiny.
6) Remove from the oven and sprinkle lightly with sea salt, if you wish.
7) Store in a tightly covered container to preserve crispness; plan to use within 1 month.

Cauliflower "Popcorn"

Here's a novel take on both cauliflower and popcorn! Little florets of crispy cauliflower take on a bright yellow, buttery hue thanks to a slightly sweet and tangy coating incorporating elements of coconut oil, honey, and curry. If your kid is an adventuresome eater, she/he might even like a tiny bit more curry added; I've intentionally kept the flavors mild. The cauliflower can be enjoyed two ways: raw or lightly roasted.

Makes 4 servings.

Ingredients:
2 tablespoons organic coconut oil
1 tablespoon locally sourced honey
¼ teaspoon sea salt
⅛ teaspoon organic curry powder
⅛ teaspoon organic turmeric, optional
2–3 cups small organic cauliflower florets

Directions:
1) Combine everything but the cauliflower in a small saucepan. Bring to a boil, then lower the heat and continue to allow it to boil and thicken for about 1 minute, stirring frequently. Watch closely, as it will burn quickly.
2) Place the cauliflower in a medium bowl. Remove the curry mixture from the heat and allow it to cool slightly before pouring over the cauliflower florets. If it is too hot, it may cause the cauliflower to "weep" a little bit of liquid.
3) Chill in the fridge to set the coating, stirring occasionally. Keep your "popcorn" refrigerated until it's time to pack it into lunchboxes. Plan to use within 4–5 days.

Tip: For a little twist on this recipe, you may wish to roast the coated cauliflower in a 400° F oven for about 20 minutes, turning occasionally. This will brown it a bit and mellow out the flavor.

Spicy Baked Chickpeas

These chickpeas, also known as garbanzo beans, take on a zesty southwest flavor in this recipe. Because they are quite savory, they may be a more popular choice among older kids. Pop a few in your kid's lunchbox for a side or snack.

Makes 3–4 servings.

Ingredients:
15.5-ounce can organic chickpeas, well drained
2 tablespoons organic olive oil
½ teaspoon sea salt
1 teaspoon organic chili powder
½ teaspoon organic cumin
¼ teaspoon organic garlic powder
2 teaspoons organic lime juice

Directions:
1) Preheat your oven to 425° F.
2) Dry the drained chickpeas with paper towels or a clean dish towel. Mix them with the olive oil and spread evenly on a baking sheet. Bake for 30 minutes, shaking or stirring once or twice. They should be fairly crunchy and golden at this point.
3) While the chickpeas are cooking, combine the sea salt, chili powder, cumin, garlic powder, and lime juice.
4) Remove the chickpeas from the oven, then drizzle or sprinkle the combined seasonings over the chickpeas, stirring to coat them evenly.
5) Bake another 3–4 minutes to evaporate the lime juice and blend the flavors. Don't overbake at this point, as the heat could burn the spices.
6) Cool completely then store in a tightly covered container in the refrigerator. Plan to use within 2 weeks.

Roasted Pumpkin Seeds

It is important to use pumpkin seeds from the edible, pie-type pumpkins when making roasted seeds. The seeds from the large, decorative pumpkins used for jack-o-lanterns have thick, tough outer coats and relatively little content in the edible centers. Not to mention, you are not as apt to find organically grown decorative pumpkins as you are organic pie pumpkins. Boiling the seeds in salt water prior to roasting them both softens the hulls and integrates the salt flavor evenly throughout the pumpkin seeds.

Ingredients:
Organic pumpkin seeds, pulled free from the flesh
Sea salt
Water

Directions:
1) Place the pumpkin seeds in whatever size saucepan fits them best. Cover them with water, measuring the water as you add it. Add 1 teaspoon of sea salt for each cup of water used. Bring the seeds to a full boil, lower the heat, and boil gently, covered, for about 30 minutes.
2) Remove the pan from the heat and allow the seeds to sit in the water until it reaches room temperature.
3) Drain them well through a strainer, and then pour the seeds evenly onto a parchment paper–lined pan.
4) Bake at 350° F for approximately 30 minutes, until the seeds are a golden light brown. Near the end of roasting time they will have a tendency to burn easily, so keep an eye on them from about 20 minutes on.
5) Remove from the oven and cool to room temperature, then store them in an airtight container for up to 1 month. For longer storage, you can freeze them for 3–4 months.

Cheese Crisps

This is one of the easiest recipes you'll ever make—and the results are so tasty! Send along for a crunchy snack or side in your kid's lunchbox.

Ingredients:
Shredded organic cheddar cheese or Parmesan cheese
Optional toppings:
Minced organic chives
Poppy seeds
Sesame seeds

Directions:
1) Preheat your oven to 400° F. Place tablespoons of the desired cheese approximately 2 inches apart on parchment paper–lined baking sheets.
2) Top with a pinch of any of the toppings you desire.
3) Bake until the cheese has melted, bubbled, and the crisps turn light golden brown Generally speaking, the Parmesan crisps will be ready a minute or two earlier than the cheddar variation. Plan on 8–10 minutes for the Parmesan and 10–12 for the cheddar. Watch closely near the end of the baking time so they don't burn.
4) Allow to cool on the sheet before gently loosening them with the wide spatula. Once cooled, they will become delightfully crispy and crunchy. Because of their high dairy content, these should be stored in the refrigerator in an airtight container. Plan to use within 1 week; sooner is better, as they may lose some of their crisp texture in the fridge.

Hummus (Seed-Free or Traditional)

I formulated this recipe in response to my school going nut- and seed-free. It was shared in our monthly nutrition newsletter so that parents could still allow their children to enjoy a classic dip without putting any of their classmates at risk. If seed consumption is not a concern, simply substitute tahini (sesame seed spread) for the soy butter in the recipe.

Ingredients:
15.5-ounce can organic chickpeas drained, reserving liquid
1 clove organic garlic, peeled and finely minced
¼ cup organic lemon juice
¾ teaspoon sea salt
2 tablespoons organic olive oil
2 tablespoons soy butter or 3 tablespoons olive oil

Directions:
1) This dip will blend fairly well in either a blender or food processor. Combine everything except the reserved canning liquid and blend or process until smooth, adding 1–2 tablespoons of the reserved liquid if necessary for consistency.
2) Refrigerate, covered, for up to 1 week, or freeze serving-size portions and store up to a month.

Tip: Hummus is particularly tasty with pita bread or pita chips, as well as veggies such as bell peppers, celery, and cucumbers.

Avocado Dip (Mild Guacamole)

I surely do love avocados—and so do many kids! This makes a creamy, smooth dip that I find very kid-friendly. The mild, bland flavor meshes nicely as a sandwich or salad component. Try blending them with just a few seasonings to make Avocado Dip. Use this mildly spiced dip to accompany Cheese Quesadillas (p. 47) or Salsa Scrambled Eggs (p. 11), as a dip for your favorite organic chips, or as a tasty substitute for mayonnaise on sandwiches.

Ingredients:
1 ripe organic Hass avocado
2–3 teaspoons organic lime or lemon juice
¼ teaspoon sea salt
¼ teaspoon organic cumin
2 tablespoons organic salsa, optional

Directions:
1) Cut the avocado in half, remove the pit, and use a spoon to scoop the flesh out of the skin. Mash with a fork, adding the lime or lemon juice, the salt, and the cumin. Adjust the flavorings to your taste.
2) Be sure to store in a small, covered container, as even with the citric acid of the juice avocados have a tendency to turn brown easily.
3) If your child has slightly more adventuresome taste buds, add in the salsa; it's an easy way to incorporate the tomatoes, onions, and other veggies frequently found in traditional guacamole.

Easy Cheese Spread

Grilled cheese sandwiches must surely rate as one of the top ten kid foods. There's nothing better than a golden, crispy, grilled-in-butter sandwich, oozing warm cheese. Unfortunately, when packed for lunchboxes, they can easily become tough and unappealing. Home-packed lunches are not the only victims of cold-grilled-cheese-sandwich syndrome. I've witnessed many an unfortunate grilled cheese disaster in the mass-produced school lunches as well—sometimes even warm tomato soup could not revive them. This cheese spread can be a valuable ally in the quest for a lunch-friendly grilled cheese sandwich. It has less tendency to harden up than sliced cheese, especially when the sandwich is not overcooked to begin with. It's also tasty as a dip for vegetables and breadsticks or a spread for crackers.

Ingredients:
2 cups (8 ounces) shredded organic cheese, such as mild cheddar or fontina
2 tablespoons organic milk
2 tablespoons organic butter, softened
1 teaspoon prepared yellow mustard
Pinch of turmeric, optional (adds color)

Directions:
1) If you have a food processor, simply combine all the ingredients and process until smooth. I've found a blender doesn't work very well for this purpose, so if you don't have a food processor, combine everything in a small pan and heat gently over low setting, stirring constantly, until the cheese just starts to melt; it should be warm, not hot, or it might separate. Remove from the heat and continue stirring or whisking until it's as smooth as you'd like.
2) Refrigerate, covered, for up to 1 week. The dip will harden when chilled, but softens somewhat when brought back to room temperature. If your child has access to a microwave oven at school, the spread can be slightly warmed to form a yummy cheese sauce that's great for dipping!

Spinach Dip

Integrating cooked spinach into this flavorful dip gives your kiddos a real nutritional boost. A kid who balks at eating a serving of cooked spinach may be more than happy to enjoy it cleverly disguised as snack food! Try serving this with whole grain crackers, rice cakes, or crusty bread, as well as the ever-popular potato chips. It's a great dip for carrot sticks or celery sticks and cucumber slices, too. Use either fresh-cooked or frozen spinach, thawed according to package directions.

Ingredients:
1 cup cooked, drained, chopped organic spinach
2 tablespoons diced organic red, orange, or yellow bell pepper*
1 teaspoon instant minced organic onion or 2 teaspoons grated fresh onion
½ teaspoon sea salt
½ teaspoon lemon pepper seasoning
¾ teaspoon dried organic dill weed or 2 teaspoons fresh snipped dill
¾ teaspoon organic parsley flakes or 2 teaspoons chopped fresh parsley
¼ cup organic mayonnaise
¼ cup organic plain Greek-style yogurt
½ cup organic sour cream

Directions:
1) Combine all the ingredients in a small bowl, stirring to blend well. This may be served right away, but tastes even better if it's allowed to mellow in the refrigerator for a little while.
2) Refrigerate leftover dip, covered, for up to a week.

If your child has an aversion to peppers, try substituting another crunchy, colorful diced vegetable, such as carrots or radishes.

Deb's Pink Radish Dip

I worked with Deb Pierotti in her third-grade classroom for several years. One thing we both enjoyed was introducing delicious and nutritious foods to the students. Her Pink Radish Dip, made with radishes the kids harvested from our class garden, was always a favorite. And as an added bonus, it contains only two ingredients!

Ingredients:
8 ounces organic cream cheese, softened
½ cup organic radishes, washed

Directions:
1) If you have a food processor, slice the tips off the washed radishes and process with the cream cheese until smooth. If you don't have a food processor, grate or finely shred the radishes and beat together with the cream cheese.
2) Serve with your favorite crackers, veggies, or chips. This also forms a great base for Open-Faced Rice Cake Sandwiches (p. 61). Yummy for lunchboxes, fancy enough for party food! Store, covered, in the fridge and plan to use within 1 week.

Edamame Pesto

Edamame (fresh soy beans) replace the more traditional pine nuts or walnuts in this bright green and flavorful pesto. This is a great recipe if your kid happens to attend a nut-free school. It can be used for dipping crackers or chips, as a spread on crusty bread, or try mixing it with hot cooked pasta for an easy-to-make main dish that can be eaten either warm or cold. For children who might find the raw garlic flavor a little too intense, try warming the minced garlic in the olive oil a minute or two to soften but not brown the garlic. Cool to room temperature before proceeding with the recipe. The amount of edamame can vary slightly, depending on what you have on hand and how stiff you would like the pesto to be.

Makes about 1 cup; number of servings varies depending on amount used per serving.

Ingredients:
2 cups lightly packed, freshly washed, organic basil leaves (remove from stems)
½– ¾ cup (fresh or frozen) cooked organic edamame
1 tablespoon finely minced organic garlic
½ cup organic olive oil
½ cup organic shredded Parmesan cheese
½ teaspoon sea salt, or to taste
A few grinds of organic black pepper, optional

Directions:
1) Place the basil and edamame in a blender or food processor and whirl until they are roughly chopped.
2) Add the rest of the ingredients and blend or process until the mixture is as smooth as you wish it to be.
3) Store, covered, in the refrigerator (the garlic smell is quite pronounced). Scoop into individual serving-size containers to pack and enjoy in any of the above ways. It also makes a tasty dip for Soft Pretzels (p. 152) or a filling for Mozzarella Cracker Stackers (p. 51).

Traditional Pesto
Prepare as for Edamame Pesto, substituting ⅓ cup organic pine nuts for the edamame and reducing the olive oil to 6 tablespoons.

Golden Sweet Potato Puree

In general, the amount of diced sweet potatoes you cook will blend down to between half and two-thirds as much puree. This versatile puree can then be used in a variety of recipes: as a component in Sweet Potato Pancakes (p. 18), Buttery Tomato Pasta Rounds (p. 103), or Rainbow Swirl Bread (p. 147), or use in place of pumpkin in Pumpkin Muffins (p. 31), Pumpkin Yogurt (p. 27), or Golden Granola (p. 36).

Ingredients:
2 cups peeled, diced organic sweet potatoes
Water to cover

Directions:
1) Place the sweet potatoes in a small or medium saucepan and add enough water just to cover the potatoes. Bring to a boil, then lower the heat and gently boil, covered, until they are very tender. Depending on the size of the sweet potato cubes, this could take between 10–20 minutes.
2) Allow the potatoes to cool slightly before draining well (reserve the cooking liquid). Blend until very smooth, adding just a bit of the cooking liquid only if necessary; you want the puree to be fairly stiff.
3) Store in a covered bowl in the fridge for 2–3 days. For longer storage time, measure set amounts and place on parchment paper–lined baking sheets. Freeze solid, then place in sealable bags or containers, label, and store in the freezer for future use.

Very Veggie Patties

Sometimes the way you present a food is as important as what you are serving. Many a kid has been known to push around the cooked vegetables on his/her plate in a furtive attempt to convince the serving adult that some really have been eaten. Here, a veritable garden of vegetables masquerade as a tasty patty to be enjoyed with another time-honored kid favorite, sour cream.

Makes 4 servings.

Ingredients:

1 cup shredded organic zucchini
½ cup shredded organic carrot
½ cup shredded organic cabbage
½ teaspoon sea salt
½ teaspoon mixed organic Italian herbs
¼ teaspoon fresh ground organic black pepper
¼ teaspoon organic garlic powder

¼ cup diced onion or 1 tablespoon organic dried onion flakes
Approximately 3 tablespoons organic olive oil
½ cup diced organic mushroom
2 tablespoons organic all-purpose flour
1 large organic egg
Organic sour cream, optional

Directions:

1) Combine the shredded zucchini, carrots, and cabbage in a mixing bowl. Add the salt, herbs, pepper, and garlic powder. If you are using dried onion flakes add those as well; stir together and set aside.
2) Heat 1 tablespoon of the oil in a large, heavy skillet or frying pan and add the diced mushroom. If you are using the fresh onion, add that now as well.
3) Sauté over medium-high heat for about 1 minute to soften and just begin to brown.
4) Add to the vegetable mixture in the bowl, stirring to combine and even out the heat.
5) Lastly, stir in the flour and the egg, making sure the white and yolk are both well combined in the mixture.
6) Heat the remaining oil over medium-high heat. Drop the veggie mixture into the hot oil in 8 even mounds, flattening slightly into a patty shape. Fry until you can see the egg beginning to cook and brown around the edges of the patties. Flip and continue to fry until the patties feel firm and they are golden on both sides. Remove from the frying pan and drain on paper towels.
7) Very Veggie Patties taste great either hot or at room temperature, served with a dollop of organic sour cream. You may find the occasional kid who prefers a bit of ketchup instead. For sandwich lovers, you can even add buns and turn them into sliders! Remember to chill when storing or sending to school.

Garnet Beet Puree

Organic beets are available throughout much of the fall and winter here in New England. When they are in stock, cook and puree some for future use. Alternatively, you can use canned organic beets, although they will produce a slightly watery and salty puree. Your garnet-colored puree can be used in a surprising variety of dishes and makes a great natural food coloring. It is a component in Can't Be Beet Chocolate Cupcakes (p. 195), Pink Whipped Potatoes (p. 97), and Peppermint Swirl Frosting (p. 191).

Ingredients:
2 cups peeled, diced organic beets
Water to cover

Directions:
1) Simply place the diced beets with enough water to cover them in a small to medium saucepan. Bring to a boil, then lower the heat and boil gently, covered, until they are quite tender. This could take 30 minutes or more, depending on the size of the beet cubes. Check occasionally to make sure the water doesn't cook down and the beets burn.
2) Once they are tender, cool slightly, and then puree the drained beets until smooth, adding just a bit of the cooking water if necessary to facilitate smooth blending; you don't want watery puree.
3) Store the puree, covered, in the fridge for 2–3 days, or freeze in premeasured amounts on a parchment paper–lined baking sheet. Once frozen, label and store in sealable bags or containers in the freezer.

Tip: Although I've seen (and used) recipes that call for baking the beets before pureeing them, I find this to be both time consuming and frustrating. The beets simply don't have enough moisture to puree smoothly, although you are welcome to try that route if you have a heavy-duty blender or food processor. They also take approximately 1 hour to bake whole, wrapped in foil.

Rainbow Swirl Bread

Here's an unusual alternative to sweet cupcakes or cookies for a special occasion treat! If you have the purees prepared in advance, it's not that complicated, but it does take a bit of time and employ some unusual techniques. It could be a fun weekend project for you and your kids to create together. Besides giving the bread its signature swirl appearance, the vegetables add flavor, moist springiness, and a nutritional boost. Try this plain or toasted, spread with butter or a bit of cream cheese, or use it as sandwich bread. The recipe is also easy to double or triple, although each loaf should still be formed individually.

Makes 1 loaf.

Ingredients:
1¾ cups organic bread flour
1 cup organic whole wheat flour
1¼ teaspoons sea salt
¼ cup lightly packed organic brown sugar
1 teaspoon organic dried onion flakes
¾ teaspoon organic dried dill weed
¼ teaspoon grated organic nutmeg
1 tablespoon active dry yeast
¼ cup Golden Sweet Potato Puree (p. 143)
¼ cup Garnet Beet Puree (p. 146)
¼ cup cooked, drained organic spinach, very finely chopped
3 tablespoons organic butter, softened, plus more for the pan
10 tablespoons organic milk, divided

Directions:
1) Combine 1 cup of the bread flour, the wheat flour, sea salt, brown sugar, dried onion, dill weed, nutmeg, and yeast, stirring or mixing with your hands to combine them very well.
2) Place the potato puree, beet puree, and spinach in three separate small saucepans or heat-proof bowls. Add 1 tablespoon of butter to each. Add 3 tablespoons of milk to the beet puree, 3 tablespoons to the sweet potato puree, and ¼ cup to the spinach.
3) Heat each mixture until very warm, but not hot; the butter will probably partially but not entirely melt.
4) Add ¾ cup of the flour mixture to each. Divide any leftover flour mixture as evenly as possible between the three. Stir each to combine well and form a stiff batter or soft dough.
5) Cover each container and allow the doughs to rise for about 1 hour in a warm place.

6) Working with one dough at a time, punch down and place on a lightly floured bread board or flat, smooth surface. Knead each with the heel of your hand until the dough is springy and pliable, adding as little additional flour as possible to keep the bread light and flavorful. Then, allow the dough to rest for about 10 minutes; this will help the gluten in it to relax and make it easier for you to roll it out.

7) While the dough rests, butter a 9-by-5-inch loaf pan.

8) Roll each section of dough separately into approximately a 9-by-18-inch rectangle, again using just a bit of flour to prevent sticking. The dough will be quite thin. You can place the rolled dough on a lightly floured baking sheet if you need the space for rolling out the other sections.

9) Stack the doughs one on top of the other, staggering the 9-inch ends slightly (each new layer showing about ½ inch of the one under it). Starting at the end where the bottom layer is peeking through, roll the dough into a spiral as tightly as you can. Place the dough, seam side down, in the buttered loaf pan. Cover loosely with a damp dish towel and allow to rise again in a warm place for 45–50 minutes, until the loaf is even or just a bit above the rim of the pan.

10) Bake in a 350° F preheated oven for 30–35 minutes, until it is golden brown and sounds hollow when tapped.

11) Remove from the oven and brush the hot top gently with butter and allow it to cool in the pan for about 5 minutes. Turn out sideways onto a cooling rack and allow to cool to room temperature . . . or at least until it's cool enough to slice without tearing. It really is delicious served warm! Use the cooled bread for sandwiches, or simply spread with butter or cream cheese. Yum!

12) Store leftovers wrapped airtight to use within a couple of days, or freeze the sliced loaf to use a little at a time.

Whole Grain Slider Buns

Younger kids in particular may not want or need an entire large sandwich for lunch. The number of them I've seen deposited in the compost or trash can attest to this. These little whole grain buns are sized just right for fun mini sandwiches or as a side to soups and salads. Older kids might like to bring a couple, possibly with a different filling in each. You'll find several suggestions in the sandwich section. Variety is the spice of life!

Makes 12 buns

Ingredients:
3 tablespoons organic honey or packed organic brown sugar
2 tablespoons organic vegetable oil
1 teaspoon sea salt
2 tablespoons flax meal
¼ cup organic rolled oats
1 cup very warm water
1 tablespoon active dry yeast
1 cup organic whole wheat flour
1¼ cups (approximately) organic bread flour

Directions:
1) Combine the honey or brown sugar, vegetable oil, salt, flax meal, rolled oats, and warm water in a large bowl, stirring to combine.
2) Sprinkle in the yeast, stirring to dissolve the yeast. Then, beat in the whole wheat flour. Cover and allow to rise in a warm place for 30 minutes.
3) Beat in 1 cup of the bread flour. Using your hands or a dough hook, add just enough of the remaining flour to form a springy dough that doesn't stick to your hands. Cover and allow the dough to rise for another 30 minutes.
4) Turn the dough out onto a smooth surface that has been dusted with a few rolled oats. Divide the dough into 12 evenly sized pieces and roll each into a small ball. Flatten each slightly in the rolled oats then place, oat side up, on a greased baking sheet, leaving some space for expansion between each. Cover with a damp dish towel and allow the dough to rise again until doubled, about 1 hour.
5) Bake in a preheated 375° F oven until the tops are golden brown and sound hollow when tapped with a knuckle, about 25 minutes.
6) Cool completely before slicing horizontally to make slider buns. The sliced buns can also be frozen for future use.

Soft Pretzels

Soft pretzels are fun to make and to eat! Don't be intimidated by shaping them or the added step of dunking them in boiling water; it's what gives them their classic, chewy finish. These are tasty served with Easy Cheese Spread (p. 137), Deb's Pink Radish Dip (p. 141) or even Hummus (p. 133). They also make a nice accompaniment to hot homemade soup or a crisp salad.

Makes 8 pretzels.

Ingredients:
2½ cups organic all-purpose flour, plus a bit more for forming pretzels
2 tablespoons packed organic brown sugar
1 teaspoon sea salt
1 tablespoon active dry yeast
1 cup very warm water
Organic oil or nonstick cooking spray, for the pan
2 cups water plus 2 tablespoons baking soda
3–4 tablespoons unsalted organic butter
Coarse sea salt

Directions:
1) Combine 1 cup of the flour, the brown sugar, salt, and yeast in a large mixing bowl and stir to combine well.
2) Pour the 1 cup of very warm water over the mixture and either blend with a dough hook or beat vigorously with a wooden spoon until it is totally smooth. Allow this batter to sit undisturbed for about 10 minutes. This allows the yeast to begin to work and the gluten in the flour to begin to develop.
3) Add in the remaining flour, again beating very well to incorporate it thoroughly. You should now have a nice springy dough. Place the bowl in a warm spot away from drafts and cover with a warm, damp dish towel. Allow to rise for 1 hour, until doubled in bulk.
4) Meanwhile, oil or spray a large baking sheet. Combine the remaining 2 cups of water with the baking soda in a small frying pan or other shallow pan, stirring to dissolve. Just before the dough has fully risen, bring the baking soda and water mixture to boiling; lower the heat while forming the pretzels.
5) Punch down the dough and divide into 8 even portions. Using a bit of flour only if necessary to prevent sticking, roll and stretch each dough section into a long, thin cord. The longer you can get it, the more classic your pretzel shape will be; I can usually stretch mine to about 18 inches. Form each cord into an open loop, twist the ends together once, leaving some of each end free, and then bring the ends up over the loop. Moisten a bit to help them stick and adhere each to form the "folded arms" of the pretzel. Place each formed pretzel on the prepared baking sheet.

6) Bring the baking soda and water back to boiling. Using a slotted spatula, lower each pretzel into the boiling water for about 5 seconds. Flip it over and place in the mixture for another 5 seconds, then carefully remove and place the pretzel back on the baking sheet. Repeat with all the pretzels. The water can now be discarded.

7) Allow the pretzels to rise again until doubled in size, about 40 minutes.

8) Adjust your oven rack to one of the upper positions, then preheat the oven to 425° F.

9) Bake the pretzels for 8–10 minutes, until they are deep golden brown. While they are baking, melt the butter over low heat.

10) Brush the cooked hot pretzels with melted butter, then sprinkle with coarse salt. Allow to cool thoroughly before bagging or storing in an airtight container.

Maple Pumpkin Rolls

I brought these delicious pumpkin rolls to our school's harvest supper one year, and they were gone in no time at all! You can also turn these into slightly larger slider buns. These are yummy as is, spread with a bit of butter, or made into your favorite ham or turkey sliders.

Makes 24 rolls.

Ingredients:

½ cup water
½ cup organic milk
¼ cup dark pure maple syrup
1¼ teaspoons sea salt
¼ cup organic butter

½ cup pureed organic pumpkin (homemade, which has more moisture than canned*)
1½ tablespoons (or 2 packets) active dry yeast
3 cups organic bread flour, approximately

Directions:

1) Heat the water, milk, syrup, salt, and butter in a small saucepan until the butter melts.
2) Remove from heat and stir in the pumpkin. Allow the mixture to cool until it is luke-warm, then stir in the yeast. Allow the yeast to work for a few minutes.
3) Beat in 1½ cups of flour, and then knead in the rest to make a smooth, elastic dough. Allow the dough to rise, covered, in a warm, damp location until doubled, about 1 hour. A tray of hot water placed under the bowl in an oven initially turned to the lowest setting and then turned off works well. (Overheating the dough would kill the yeast, turning your rolls into hard, flat lumps).
4) Punch down the dough with your fist and turn out onto a flat, lightly floured surface. If you have the correct amount of flour in the dough, it should be springy but not sticky. Don't add extra flour if you don't need to; it will turn your rolls tough and flavorless!
5) Form the dough into 24 rolls and place them in two 8- or 9-inch round or one 9-by-13-inch buttered cake pan. For sliders, form the dough into 12–18 slightly larger rolls instead. In this case I would recommend placing the dough mounds on buttered baking sheets, flattening them slightly, and leaving space between each for expansion before the second rising. For a little extra touch, try brushing the tops of the rolls lightly with milk or beaten egg and sprinkling with hulled pumpkin seeds prior to baking.
6) Allow the dough to rise until doubled, about 45 minutes.
7) Bake in a preheated 375° F oven until golden brown and hollow sounding when tapped; start checking between 20–25 minutes, depending on the size of the rolls.
8) When they're done cooking, brush the warm tops of the rolls generously with butter. Carefully turn out of the pan after 5–10 minutes to cool completely on wire racks, or serve warm from the oven. For sliders, gently remove to cooling racks with a spatula, then cool completely before slicing each in half horizontally.

If you are using canned pumpkin puree rather than fresh, you may wish to replace 1–2 tablespoons of it with water, as the canned will be more dense than home pureed.

Baking Powder Biscuits

It is important that the butter or coconut oil is well chilled for this recipe. If it's difficult to measure the coconut oil when it's too hard, you can soften it a bit for that purpose and then stick it in the freezer for a few minutes to harden prior to constructing the biscuits. These make dandy little breakfast sandwiches. Try filling them with a cooked Maple Sausage Patty (p. 13) or Slightly Spicy Sausage Patty (p. 12), along with a firmly fried egg and/or a slice or organic cheese, or just use the egg and cheese. Vary by spreading with a bit of fruit spread and cream cheese, or substitute natural ham or bacon for the sausage. You can also vary the size of the biscuits you cut according the size and appetites of the children involved.

Makes 6–8 biscuits.

Ingredients:
2 cups organic all-purpose flour
4 teaspoons baking powder
1 teaspoon sea salt
1 teaspoon organic sugar
⅓ cup organic coconut oil or 6 tablespoons organic unsalted butter
¾—1 cup organic milk

Directions:
1) Place your oven rack in one of the top positions (you don't want the biscuit bottoms to burn), then preheat the oven to 450° F.
2) Combine all the dry ingredients in a medium mixing bowl. Using a fork, 2 knives, a pastry cutter, or your fingers, work in the coconut oil or butter until there are crumbles the size of small peas throughout. An easy shortcut for this is simply to shred the cold butter into the flour mixture using a cheese or vegetable grater.
3) Add in the milk and stir lightly to blend. For a more tender biscuit you can add slightly more milk (up to 1 cup total). This makes the dough softer and a little trickier to knead, but if it stands for a minute it will firm up.
4) Turn the dough out onto a floured board and gently fold it over a few times; this incorporates layers that will help with the flakiness factor. Pat the dough out to a ½-inch thickness; if you plan to split the biscuits for sandwiches, make the dough a little thicker. Cut into circles or squares.
5) Place the biscuits on an ungreased baking sheet and bake for about 10 minutes, until risen and light golden brown.
6) I find the biscuits are generally a little easier to split simply by pulling gently apart when they are still warm, although you can also cut them in half using a serrated knife once they have cooled. Biscuits do not store particularly well; place them in a covered container in the fridge for 2–3 days if need be. You can also wrap them

and freeze for up to 1 month, although they do have a tendency to dry out easily. Making them into breakfast sandwiches and wrapping individually prior to freezing is a good alternative. They will thaw out on their own in the lunchbox.

Tip: If you want less waste dough (you can always pat out extra and cut again, but the biscuits are never as nice as the others), try patting into a square or rectangle. Trim just a thin strip from the edges, so they rise properly when baking, and then cut the dough into squares. Bake as above.

Homemade Graham Crackers

Graham flour is simply whole wheat flour that contains more of the wheat germ. I use Bob's Red Mill organic graham flour. If you cannot find graham flour, simply substitute any good-quality organic whole wheat flour. These graham crackers contain brown sugar and a touch of honey for that classic taste. Add in the optional bit of cinnamon if you prefer cinnamon grahams.

Yield will vary depending on the size of your crackers.

Ingredients:

1½ cups organic graham flour
1 cup organic all-purpose flour
½ teaspoon baking soda
½ teaspoon baking powder
½ teaspoon cinnamon, optional
½ cup organic butter, softened

¼ cup organic coconut oil, partially melted
½ cup lightly packed organic brown sugar
2 tablespoons locally sourced honey
¾ teaspoon organic vanilla extract
⅓ cup organic milk

Directions:

1) Place your oven rack in one of the top positions, then preheat the oven to 350° F.
2) Combine the graham flour, all-purpose flour, baking soda, baking powder, and cinnamon, if using, in a medium bowl; set it aside.
3) In a large mixing bowl, cream together the butter, coconut oil, brown sugar, honey, and vanilla until it's light and fluffy.
4) Add in approximately half the flour mixture, mixing on low speed until well combined. Add the milk and mix again. Finally, add the remaining flour mixture. The dough will appear somewhat crumbly, but should hold together and form into a ball. If it seems too crumbly, carefully add another tablespoon or so of milk.
5) Roll out half the dough at a time on a lightly floured board to about ⅛ inch thick. Cut the dough into 2 to 3-inch squares, using a pizza cutter, pastry cutter, or a sharp knife.
6) Place the crackers on ungreased baking sheets and prick the top of each one with a fork.
7) Bake for 15 minutes, until the crackers are just beginning to brown around the edges. Remove carefully with a broad spatula to cool on wire racks. Store in an airtight container and plan to use within 2–3 weeks.

Tip: If you want to make some fun cracker shapes, try cutting them out with a variety of cookie cutters!

Pie Crust Cheese Crackers

This is another handy way to use up extra pie crust dough, or you can make the dough specifically for these. Use the Buttery Pie Crust recipe in the Breakfast for Lunch chapter or experiment with another favorite pie crust recipe. I've found rolling out a half batch of the dough gives you the most manageable amount to deal with at a time, so the other ingredients are listed proportionate to that amount. It's easy to multiply them accordingly if you prefer to make more crackers at once.

Makes 24 crackers.

Ingredients:
¼ teaspoon organic paprika
¼ teaspoon sea salt
⅛ teaspoon dry mustard
Flour for rolling purposes
½ batch Buttery Pie Crust dough (p. 21), chilled
½ cup finely shredded organic cheddar cheese

Directions:
1) Place your oven rack in the upper position, then preheat the oven to 375° F.
2) Combine the paprika, salt, and mustard in a small bowl; set aside.
3) Lightly flour a hard, flat surface. Roll the chilled dough into a rectangle that's approximately 6 by 12 inches, with the long side facing you.
4) Lightly dab a small amount of water over the surface to help facilitate the flavorings and cheese adhering. Then, using your fingers for control, evenly sprinkle the dried seasonings over two-thirds of the surface. Sprinkle the cheese on top of the seasonings, pressing down into the surface of the dough.
5) Next, take the section of dough with no cheese on it and fold it over the middle third of the dough and press it down. Now take the folded portion and fold it once again over the remaining third, bringing it even with the far edge. Turn the dough so that the long side is again facing you.
6) Roll out to a rectangle again and once again fold the dough in thirds, flouring both sides of the dough lightly to prevent sticking as necessary. Then roll out the dough one more time.
7) Cut the crackers into 1- to 1½-inch squares and place them on a parchment paper–lined baking sheet.
8) Bake for approximately 25 minutes, until the crackers are puffed, deep golden brown, and have become uniformly crisp.
9) Allow to cool to room temperature before storing in a tightly covered container. The crackers should be good for up to 2 weeks, although because of their high cheese and dairy content, they may grow stale easily, especially in hot weather.

Oatcakes

Oatcakes are very popular in Scotland (birthplace of one of my grandmothers) as well as in Scotland's western counterpart, Nova Scotia. Traditional Scottish oatcakes are apt to contain rolled oats, a bit of salt and fat, and not much else. Nova Scotian oatcakes are slightly sweet, softer, and more complex—and probably more kid-friendly, too. These oatcakes are particularly tasty with a bit of butter and/or fruit spread. Cheese is also a good accompaniment, and easy to pack with the oatcakes for a simple lunch entrée.

Makes approximately 18 oatcakes.

Ingredients:
1½ cups organic all-purpose flour
2 cups organic rolled oats
½ cup lightly packed organic brown sugar
½ teaspoon baking soda
½ teaspoon sea salt
½ cup cold organic butter
⅓ cup organic buttermilk or ⅓ cup organic milk plus ½ teaspoon vinegar

Directions:
1) Place your oven rack in one of the top positions, then preheat the oven to 375° F.
2) Combine the flour, rolled oats, brown sugar, baking soda, and salt in a large mixing bowl. Shred in the cold butter, mixing lightly, or cut it into fine cubes and work it in with your fingers. Stir in the buttermilk or the milk/vinegar mixture.
3) Turn half the dough out onto a very lightly floured board and pat out to approximately ¼ inch thick. Cut with a round cookie cutter or other round object; I use the top of a drinking glass. Remove carefully to an ungreased baking sheet. Repeat with the second half of the dough.
4) Bake for 15 minutes, until the cakes are slightly puffed and light brown around the edges. Allow to cool slightly before carefully loosening them from the pan. Once they have entirely cooled, pack for lunches or store in an airtight container. These are best eaten within 2–3 days.

Desserts

Too Sweet . . . or Not Too Sweet?

How much added sugar children consume certainly is a concern. According to American Heart Association guidelines, kids aged 2 to 18 should consume no more than 6 teaspoons of added sugar on a daily basis. Excess sugar consumption has been linked to childhood obesity and a predisposition to health problems, including diabetes and heart disease.

Added sugar is categorized as any natural sweetening agent, from granulated sugar to molasses to honey, that is added to foods. Fresh fruit or 100 percent fruit juices do not contain added sugar. However, canned or frozen fruits in sugar syrup do. Sugar-sweetened juice blends, "power drinks," and carbonated beverages are among the worst culprits.

With that in mind, there is still no denying that sugar-sweetened foods are pervasive in our diets for one obvious reason: they taste good. And many children's snack foods are marketed with that in mind.

Here I offer several approaches to the sugar conundrum. There are recipes for fruit-based desserts with no added sugar and for familiar desserts, such as gelatin and pudding, that either do not contain added sugar or contain less sugar than their commercial counterparts, as well as no preservatives, additives, or artificial flavors. Finally, although there are a few unabashedly sweet offerings for special occasions, even these come with what I like to think of as redeeming qualities. And now you have the opportunity to make and enjoy them using organic ingredients!

Fruit Gel Cups

Those little cups of colored gelatin studded with pieces of fruit hold lots of kid appeal, but also an overload of sugar and artificial coloring. Try these tasty alternatives instead. Although I cannot find organic gelatin powder locally in my small hometown, it is readily available online. Make sure you buy gelatin that is intended for gelling purposes; some gelatin that is sold as a nutritional supplement may not gel properly.

Purchasing a couple packages of small food storage cups with lids will provide you with a handy supply of reusable gel containers. You can also pour the gelatin mixture into a lightly oiled square baking pan and cut into serving-size squares once it's set; easy to fit into a sandwich container! Or simply chill in a bowl and spoon out individual servings as needed.

Lemon-Lime Gel with Blueberries

Using apple juice in place of water allows you to add less sugar while still mellowing the tartness of the lemon and lime juice. You can also use only lemon or only lime juice, if you prefer. Blueberries added to the partially set gel add a pretty contrast and tasty flavor as well as a nutritional boost.

Makes 4 servings.

Ingredients:
2½ teaspoons (1 packet) unflavored gelatin powder
¼ cup organic sugar
2 tablespoons organic lemon juice
2 tablespoons organic lime juice
1¾ cups organic apple juice
1 cup organic blueberries

Directions:
1) Combine the gelatin powder and sugar in a small bowl. Pour the lemon and lime juice over this mixture, stirring to combine well.
2) Allow the gelatin to soften while you heat ¾ cup of the apple juice just to boiling in a small saucepan. Stir in the gelatin mixture, making sure to scrape it all in, and stir until it is completely dissolved. Remove from the heat and stir in the remaining cup of apple juice.
3) Pour the mixture into a bowl and chill in the refrigerator until partially set but still soft. Fold in the blueberries and divide the gel mixture evenly among the individual containers.
4) Chill until set, snap on the lids, and store in the refrigerator until ready to pack for lunch.

Fruited Raspberry Gel

Using fresh or frozen raspberries takes a little more effort than pouring juice from a bottle, but the results are much more colorful and flavorful. The little bit of water or apple juice used helps mellow out the raspberry flavor, allowing you to use less sugar while still producing a pleasingly sweet gel. Combining the raspberry gel with peaches is a classic, although pears are quite tasty, too. Note that the natural red of the raspberries tends to color whatever fruit has been added. For an especially raspberry-filled treat, try adding some whole raspberries instead!

Makes 4 servings.

Ingredients:
2½ cups fresh or frozen organic raspberries
1¼ cups water or organic apple juice
¼ cup organic sugar (if you add raspberries, you may want just a bit more)
2½ teaspoons (1 packet) unflavored gelatin powder
1 cup fresh, frozen, or canned organic diced peaches or pears, well drained, or 1 cup fresh or frozen, partially thawed organic raspberries

Directions:
1) Combine the 2½ cups of raspberries and 1 cup of water or apple juice in a medium saucepan. Bring just to a boil, crushing the berries slightly with the back of a spoon.
2) Remove from the heat and pour the mixture through a sieve into a bowl or liquid measuring cup to remove the raspberry seeds. If you press the mixture you will get a little more of the raspberry solids, but your gel will also be cloudier. Discard the seeds in the sieve and measure the liquid; there should be about 1¾ cups. Add a bit of water if need be to make the full amount.
3) Put 1 cup of this juice in a bowl and set aside; pour the rest back into the pan and stir in the sugar.
4) Place the gelatin in a small bowl and add ¼ cup of water or juice, then stir to blend. Allow it to soften while heating the sugar and raspberry juice over medium-high heat just to boiling. Scrape the softened gelatin into the pan and stir until it is thoroughly dissolved. Remove from the heat and stir in the remaining juice.
5) Pour the entire mixture back into the bowl and refrigerate until it is chilled and soft-set. Then, stir in the diced fruit or whole raspberries. Divide evenly among the individual serving cups and chill until it is totally set. Snap on the lids and store in the refrigerator until ready to pack.

Orange-Pineapple Sunshine Gel

I experimented with a few different juice combinations for this, not quite getting the flavor I wanted without adding sugar. I eventually decided that investing in a flavorful organic juice blend was the best way to go. The one I settled on combines orange and pineapple juices with white grape and carrot. If you already have a family favorite, give it a try in this sunny fruit gel. Whatever combination you decide upon, be sure to use canned pineapple juice, as fresh or frozen pineapple contains an enzyme that will prevent your gelatin from gelling—where's the fun in that? Add in whatever combination of fruit and carrots you'd like. You can also leave it plain and serve with some fresh berries on the side.

Makes 4 servings.

Ingredients:
Organic canned crushed pineapple, orange sections, and/or organic shredded carrot
2 cups organic orange-pineapple juice blend (or less if using canned fruit, optional)
2½ teaspoons (1 packet) unflavored gelatin powder

Directions:
1) If you are using canned fruit, drain it very well. If you wish, measure the canned fruit juice and use it as part of the gel base. Add the juice blend to the canned fruit juice to total 2 cups, or simply use all juice blend. Set 1 cup of the juice aside.
2) Soften the gelatin in ¼ cup of the remaining juice. Meanwhile, heat ¾ cup of the juice to just under boiling in a small saucepan. Add the softened gelatin, stirring until it has completely dissolved. Remove from the heat and stir in the cup of reserved juice.
3) Refrigerate or chill over ice water until it cools and thickens slightly. Fold in whatever combination of fruit and/or carrots you wish. Pour into individual containers, snap on the lids, and store in the refrigerator until ready to pack.

Double Grape Gel

One little girl who tried this for the first time declared, "This is the best thing ever in my whole life!" And that is probably the most amazing endorsement ever in my whole life! The natural sweetness of the grape juice and grapes contribute mightily to the tastiness factor of Double Grape Gel. I have found that Santa Cruz organic grape juice has a really nice flavor. Look for smaller grapes if at all possible; they fit in more evenly and are easier to spoon out while eating. Organic grapes are sometimes difficult to find. One alternative you may wish to explore are grapes labeled as Rainforest Alliance Certified. Although I don't believe these are organic, they do represent sustainable agriculture and fair labor practices in the regions where they are grown.

Makes 4 servings.

Ingredients:
2 cups organic pure grape juice
1 packet unflavored gelatin powder (2½ teaspoons)
1 cup seedless organic grapes, rinsed well

Directions:
1) Place 1 cup of the grape juice in a small bowl and set aside. Place another ¾ cup of the grape juice into a small saucepan and heat to just boiling. While that juice is heating, soften the gelatin in the remaining ¼ cup of juice.
2) Once the juice in the pan has reached boiling, quickly stir in all the gelatin and remove the pan from the heat. Continue stirring until the gelatin has completely dissolved.
3) Stir the heated mixture into the juice in the bowl.
4) Chill the liquid gelatin by placing the bowl in a larger bowl of ice water or in the freezer until it becomes semi-congealed. At this point, fold in the grapes and pour into your desired serving containers. Refrigerate until firm.

Strawberry Chewies

The only ingredient in these delectable little tidbits is fresh, organic strawberries. It's a nice way to give them longer life when they're in season or on special at the store. The slow process of baking at a low temperature removes excess moisture, rendering them sweet and chewy. Plan on dehydrating them on a day when you're going to be around the house. Although they can be left for an hour or so at a time, they do require some minimal attention at intervals. This recipe includes two separate time variations; the first for juicer, chewy berries that should be refrigerated and eaten fairly quickly, the second for drier berries that can be stored for a longer period of time at room temperature.

Ingredients:
Organic strawberries

Directions:
1) Wash the berries well, shaking off any excess moisture.
2) Place your oven rack in the middle position and preheat the oven to 200° F.
3) Remove the stems and leaves from each berry, scooping out a tiny bit at the top. If the berries are quite small (thumbnail size), you can leave them whole; otherwise cut them from top to bottom into two even halves.
4) Place the berries, cut side up, on a parchment paper–lined baking sheet or sheets; make sure there is a bit of room between each berry for air to circulate. Place in the preheated oven and leave without disturbing for 2 hours.
5) After 2 hours, gently redistribute the strawberries, turning over whole ones and placing the halved berries cut side down. Bake the berries for 1 more hour.
   At this point, they will not be fully dehydrated but will be soft and almost gummy to touch. If you wish to enjoy your berries in this form, they can now be removed from the oven. Although they are quite tasty this way, not enough of the strawberry juices have been dehydrated out of them for long-term storage. Plan to use these strawberries within 2–3 days, refrigerating what you don't use right away.
6) To further dry the berries and render them safe to store, simply leave them in the oven for another 2½–3 hours, shaking the pan occasionally to keep the drying process even. After this they will still be pliable, but they will have flattened out and will not feel sticky when picked up. Allow them to cool thoroughly before placing in sealable bags or storage jars. An important step to take if you plan to store your berries for any length of time is to shake them around in the jar and check for any excess moisture. If you detect any, simply pop them back into the oven, again at 200° F, for another half hour or so. Remember, strawberries that have retained some excess moisture will be prone to mold and spoilage.

Pear Bunnies

Pear halves form the bunnies in question, nested on a blanket of pink fruity yogurt. I first came across a recipe for "Blushing Bunnies" when I was a kid in 4-H, back in the 1960s. In that recipe, the little pear bunnies were lightly sprinkled with fruit-flavored red gelatin powder to give them their blush. These bunnies might not be blushing, but they sure are healthier and tastier!

Ingredients:
Organic fruit yogurt of choice, such as raspberry, strawberry, or cherry
Organic canned pear halves, well drained*
Sliced organic almonds**
Organic dried cranberries
Organic whipped cream
Organic fresh berries of choice

Directions:
1) Smooth some yogurt over the bottom of a fairly flat bowl that has a tight-fitting lid. Center the pear, cut side down, on top.
2) Add sliced almond ears, bits of dried cranberry for the eyes and nose, and a little rosette of whipped cream for the bunny tail. Pipe some more cream around the edges and decorate with more almonds, dried cranberries, and fresh berries.
3) Make sure to send with an iced gel pack, and hopefully a way to keep it level during transport. An upside-down bunny will still taste just as good, it just won't look quite itself.

*Although canned pears work best for this, you can use fresh ripe pears that have been peeled, halved, and cored. Brush with a little diluted lemon juice to help prevent browning.
** If your child cannot tolerate tree nuts, or your school doesn't allow them, simply omit the almonds. Perhaps your bunny would like thinly sliced strawberry ears instead.

Mango Yum-Yums

Mango Yum-Yums are even easier to make than Strawberry Chewies. Once you pop them in the oven, you need only loosen and turn them once or twice in the next couple of hours, and voilà! You have a tray of sweet, chewy, all-natural treats to snack on or send as a tasty alternative to sugar-sweetened lunch desserts.

Ingredients:
Organic mangoes, washed and peeled
Sprinkle of organic lemon or lime juice, optional

Directions:
1) Place your oven rack in one of the top positions and preheat the oven to 200° F.
2) Slice each mango from top to bottom around the large seed in the middle, cutting out thin wedges. You want these nice and thin; I average 20 slices per mango.
3) Place the slices in rows, with a bit of space between each, on parchment paper-lined baking sheets. If you wish, you may sprinkle each slice with just a few drops of lemon or lime juice. I simply squeeze a few drops from a fresh cut half of lemon or lime, although this step isn't really necessary.
4) Bake for 1 hour, then carefully lift and turn each slice over. They have a slight tendency to stick, so try not to burn your fingertips in the process! Continue baking another 1–1½ hours, until the slices are fairly dry but still somewhat pliable. Turn off the oven and allow them to cool completely while still on the baking sheets in the oven. I'm not sure exactly how long these will successfully store, as I've always eaten them almost immediately! They should be good in a covered container for up to 1 week. I would advise storing in the fridge, although they are fine to send for lunch at room temperature.

Banana-mobiles

Use baby bananas for these cute little cars. If you can't find organic baby bananas, you can cut larger bananas in half. Brushing a bit of orange or lemon juice on the bananas will help prevent them from browning, although the uncut surfaces are fairly resistant to this.

Ingredients:
Organic baby bananas, peeled
Organic kiwi, peeled and cut in slices
Organic blueberries, well rinsed
Wooden toothpicks
Organic bunny cookies or graham crackers
Cupcake liners for "parasols," optional

Directions:
1) Construct the banana-mobiles by skewering a kiwi slice and a blueberry for each wheel; run one toothpick through the front and one through the back of the banana, attaching a "wheel" to either side.
2) Hull a large strawberry and cut out a little seat in it; skewer to the top of the banana-mobile with another toothpick.
3) Perch a bunny in the driver's seat. Add a cupcake liner and toothpick parasol, decorated with a blueberry or two, if you wish.

Tip: For safety, be sure to remove all toothpicks before serving to young children.

Stuffed Apples

Almost any kind of crisp, juicy apple will do for this recipe. There are numerous fillings that can be used for them; the classic peanut butter and raisins is the one I've seen most over the years. However, there are all sorts of tasty alternatives to that old standby if your child can't tolerate peanut butter or the school doesn't allow it. A few stuffing suggestions are listed below.

Plan on ½–1 apple for each serving, depending on the size and appetite of your child.

Ingredients:
Whole organic apples
Filling of choice:
Organic soy butter or sunflower seed or nut butter; organic raisins, organic cinnamon, optional
Organic chocolate hazelnut spread; organic nuts of choice (walnuts, almonds, hazelnuts, etc.)*
Organic cream cheese; locally produced honey, organic cinnamon, or organic vanilla extract

Directions:
1) Wash the apples, cut them in half, and remove the cores.
2) Choose your filling, then begin with 2 tablespoons of the first ingredient. Add 1 tablespoon of the second ingredient. Accent with a sprinkle of cinnamon or ¼ teaspoon of vanilla, if called for. Cream together well.
3) Fill the hollows in each apple half with the filling of choice. Fit the apple back together again or leave the halves separate, if you prefer. Remember that the apple flesh will darken upon exposure to air.
4) Wrap or place in a covered container for transporting to school.

Obviously, choose option #2 only if your child can tolerate tree nuts and/or your school allows them.

Wild Rice Pudding

This simple pudding was created as part of our third grade Native American studies one year. Cranberries, blueberries, and fox grapes (tart dark grapes similar to Concord grapes) are the three "original" fruits of New England, so it seemed only fitting to combine them with wild rice and pure maple syrup, two more north American originals. I'm fortunate to have a son in Minnesota who sends me packets of wild rice grown and harvested in the northern part of that state. The latest one is from the Red Lake Nation of the Chippewa. You may want to check out your whole food stores, co-ops, or online to find a good source for yourself. Send a small container of this to school for an unusual and healthy end to your child's lunch.

Makes 4–6 servings.

Ingredients:
½ cup wild rice
2 cups water
¼ cup pure maple syrup, or to taste
¼ cup dried organic cranberries
heaping ¼ cup organic blueberries, preferably wild
¼ cup organic raisins

Directions:
1) Combine the wild rice and water in a small saucepan with a tight-fitting lid. Bring to a boil, then reduce the heat to low and simmer, covered, for 30–40 minutes, until the rice is tender and the water is mostly absorbed. Turn off the heat and leave the rice to cool slightly; it will absorb more of the water as it cools.
2) Stir in the maple syrup, berries, and the raisins.
3) Serve the pudding warm or at room temperature. Divide into individual serving containers for transport to school. A gel pack to keep the pudding cool until lunch is always a good idea.

Tip: For this recipe, the blueberries can be fresh, frozen, or dried, but do get the wild ones if you can find them. Wild blueberries are smaller with a more pronounced flavor than their domestic counterparts. They are also higher in antioxidants and nutrients. Fresh cranberries, on the other hand, are too tart and crunchy to eat raw, so used dried instead.

Chocolate Pudding Cups

Chocolate pudding is a dessert dear to the heart of many a kid. This homemade organic version is smooth and creamy without any of the additives commercial pudding cups often contain. Pour the cooked pudding directly into serving containers for the smoothest presentation. It can also be stored in a larger bowl and spooned out when desired, possibly smoothed over with a bit of Chocolate Whipped Cream. Top it off with strawberries, raspberries, or sweet cherries if you wish.

Makes 4–6 servings.

Ingredients:
¼ cup organic cornstarch
¼ cup organic cocoa powder
½ cup organic sugar
2 cups organic milk (whole milk is best, but any will do)
1 tablespoon organic butter
1 teaspoon organic vanilla extract
Whipped cream or Chocolate Whipped Cream (p. 196), optional, for topping

Directions:
1) Put the cornstarch, cocoa powder, and sugar into a medium saucepan. Using a whisk, stir them together until well combined. Stir in the milk and butter. Don't worry, the butter will melt while you're cooking the pudding.
2) Turn the heat to medium and cook the pudding, stirring with the whisk or a spoon to keep it from sticking to the bottom of the pan, until it comes to a full boil. Turn off the heat and stir in the vanilla.
3) Let it cool slightly before pouring into desired serving containers, and then chill it in the refrigerator until it is cold. Pudding forms a sticky "skin" on the top when it cools. If you don't want that, put a piece of wax paper or plastic wrap directly on top of the pudding while it's cooling and take it off when you're ready to eat it. (I don't think I'd worry about this once it's in the individual containers.)
4) When ready to eat, top with whipped cream if desired. You can easily top the chilled pudding with the cream before sending it to school. Try to position it so the contents stay right side up, if possible, and be sure to keep it all cold with a gel pack!

Arroz Con Leche

Arroz con leche translates very simply as "rice with milk," and is based on a recipe the kids in my reading group and I discovered in one of our books about Guatemala. It is a simple rice pudding flavored with cinnamon and orange peel and works very nicely as a pudding cup for school snack or dessert.

Makes 6–8 servings.

Ingredients:
2½ cups organic milk (whole milk works best)
½ cup organic white rice, preferably jasmine
¼ cup organic sugar
1 organic cinnamon stick
Thin strip of organic orange peel, about 8 inches long, or ½ teaspoon organic orange extract
Small pinch of sea salt
1 tablespoon organic butter
Organic ground cinnamon for topping, optional

Directions:
1) Combine everything except the ground cinnamon in a medium saucepan with a tight-fitting lid. Bring to a boil over medium heat, stirring frequently to prevent sticking.
2) Reduce the heat to the lowest setting and cook, covered, for 15–20 minutes, stirring occasionally.
3) Turn off the heat, cover tightly, and allow it to sit for about 1 hour, until most of the liquid has absorbed.
4) Stir again and remove the orange peel and cinnamon stick.
5) This may be served warm or chilled, although for school lunches you'll want to spoon it into individual serving containers and refrigerate until it's time to send to school. Sprinkle with a bit of cinnamon, if you wish, for topping, or add a small dollop of whipped cream for a special treat. Be sure to send with a gel pack to keep it cool.

Cherry Egg Rolls

My penchant for the improbable combination of cherries in an egg roll wrap originated many moons ago, when those amazing inventions referred to as TV dinners were in their infancy. One labeled "Chinese" included a generic entrée I no longer remember, flanked on one side by a vegetable egg roll, and for dessert, on the other side, was an egg roll filled with sweetened tart cherries. I do wish organic tart cherries were more readily available; they are a powerhouse of antioxidants, not to mention darn delicious! Because the only tart cherries available locally to me are canned, non-GMO (but not organic), I've included two filling variations: one with tart cherries, the other with frozen, organic sweet cherries. In either case, if you wish to be adventuresome, I've also included directions for making your own egg roll wrappers. Again, these are not readily available to me in organic form. No matter how you end up concocting them, Cherry Egg Rolls provide a refreshing contrast to the trans-fat-laden, artificially colored and flavored cherry hand pies often sold with kid's lunchboxes in mind.

Makes 8–16 egg rolls.

Tart Cherry Filling
Ingredients:
14.5-ounce can tart red cherries
½ cup organic sugar
2½ tablespoons organic cornstarch
½ teaspoon organic almond extract
¼ teaspoon organic cinnamon

Directions:
1) Drain the cherry juice into a medium saucepan and set the cherries aside. Add the sugar, cornstarch, almond extract, and cinnamon, then stir until smooth.
2) Bring to a boil over medium heat, stirring to prevent burning. Gently stir in the cherries and reheat just to boiling, being careful so the delicate cherries don't break apart.
3) Remove from the heat and cool completely before filling the egg roll wrappers.

Sweet Cherry Filling
Ingredients:
8-ounce package frozen sweet dark cherries, approximately 1½ cups
½ cup water
1 tablespoon lemon juice
¼ cup organic sugar
2 tablespoons organic cornstarch

½ teaspoon organic almond extract
¼ teaspoon organic cinnamon

Directions:
1) Combine all the ingredients in a medium saucepan. Bring to a full boil over medium heat, stirring to prevent burning.
2) Remove from the heat and cool completely before filling the egg roll wrappers.

Egg Roll Wrapper Dough
Ingredients:
2 cups organic all-purpose flour
½ teaspoon sea salt
1 large organic egg
½ cup cold water
Having a food processor or heavy-duty mixer with a dough hook will make this recipe much easier.

Directions:
1) Combine all ingredients in the bowl of a stand mixer or processor and mix or blend until it is smooth, elastic, and pulls away from the edges into a cohesive lump.
2) Place in a plastic storage bag or container with a tight-fitting lid and store in the fridge until you're ready to form your egg rolls, but not more than 2–3 days.

Note: *This recipe makes enough dough for 16 egg roll wrappers, enough for a double batch of filling, if you wish. Extra uncooked wrappers can be refrigerated, well-floured, and separated by bits of parchment paper, for 2–3 days if sealed to keep them from drying out. Freeze them for longer-term storage. Store the cooked egg rolls, covered, in the fridge.*

Cherry Egg Rolls
Ingredients:
Egg Roll Wrapper Dough or commercially produced egg roll wrappers
Desired cherry filling
Organic flour for the pan
Organic vegetable oil for frying
Organic confectioners' sugar

Directions:
1) Divide the egg roll dough into 4 even portions. Roll out the dough, one portion at a time, on a lightly floured board until it measures approximately 12 by 12 inches. This will take quite a bit of rolling. Cut each square into 4 smaller ones.
2) Place approximately one-eighth of your chosen filling (the tart cherry makes a bit more, so you might get an extra egg roll or two from it) on one of the dough squares, about ⅓ inch away from one edge. If your square is perfectly symmetrical, you can roll

it in the typical egg roll fashion of two corners over (in a diamond shape), and then rolling from the closer end point over, sealing the final point with a dab of water. If they're not even, you can turn the two side edges toward the center and then roll, again affixing the final flap with water. The only disadvantage to this method is that you'll have thicker walls to the wrapper in some places than others, which will affect frying time. Whichever way you choose to form them, the most important step is making sure the filling is sealed very well inside the egg roll, as the sugar will burn during frying if it seeps out.

3) Place each formed egg roll, seam side down, on a parchment paper–lined baking sheet that has been dusted generously with flour to prevent sticking.

4) Put about 1 cup of the oil in a heavy skillet (I use a medium cast-iron skillet) and put it over medium-high heat for 5–10 minutes before frying. Fry the egg rolls, turning over as necessary, until golden brown. Remove from the pan with a slotted spatula, then drain on paper towels. If you prefer to use a deep fat fryer, follow the directions on the appliance and heat the oil to 375° F, frying the egg rolls to a golden brown before draining on paper towels.

5) Sprinkle the egg rolls lightly with confectioners' sugar, if you wish, or save that step until just before sending for lunch. Do not try eating one until they have cooled; the filling will be very hot!

Tip: Instead of rolling the dough, you can also gently pull it wider and thinner using your fingers; it is quite elastic, but you do want to be careful not to pull it too thin or to tear a hole in it. If you do, dab a little water on the torn edges and glue them back together, dusting with flour as needed to prevent sticking.

Banana Bread with Chocolate Chips

Sometimes we would get some overripe bananas as part of our school healthy snack program. Rather than letting them go to waste, I would bring them home and make banana bread, which is always a big hit with the primary grade crowd. Occasionally, for a special touch, I'd add chocolate chips, making a decadent but not over-the-top treat to be enjoyed by all!

Makes 2 loaves.

Ingredients:
3 ripe bananas, peeled and mashed (about 1½ cups)
½ cup organic vegetable oil
1 cup organic sugar
2 large organic eggs
2 cups organic all-purpose flour
1 teaspoon baking soda
½ teaspoon sea salt
½ teaspoon baking powder
¼ cup organic milk
1 teaspoon organic vanilla extract
½ teaspoon organic lemon flavoring, optional
½ –1 cup organic chocolate chips, optional
Organic butter and flour for the pan

Directions:
1) Preheat the oven to 350° F.
2) In a large mixing bowl beat together the bananas, oil, sugar, and eggs until the mixture is fairly smooth.
3) In a separate bowl, combine the flour, baking soda, salt, and baking powder. Add about half of this to the banana mixture and blend well. Add the milk and flavorings and beat again. Finally, beat in the rest of the flour mixture until everything is nice and smooth. Stir in the chocolate chips.
4) Pour the batter evenly into two greased and floured 9-by-5-inch loaf tins. Bake for 45–50 minutes, until the loaves have risen and the tops are golden, cracked appearing, and firm to touch. Insert a toothpick if you are not sure; it should come out mostly clean. Cool in the pans for 5–10 minutes, then gently turn out sideways onto cooling racks. Don't try to slice until the loaves have cooled to room temperature or they will crumble and fall apart.
5) Serve just as is, or with a bit of butter or cream cheese.

Peppermint Swirl Frosting

Put this frosting on the Can't Be Beet Chocolate Cupcakes (p. 195) for a treat that tastes even better than cupcakes you might get from a bakery! The peppermint swirl effect comes from striping a small amount of bright pink frosting up one side of a pastry bag before adding the white frosting. Use a large star tip to swirl concentric circles of frosting onto each cupcake. Perfect for seasonal parties, winter birthdays, or anytime your kid deserves a special treat!

Makes enough to frost 24 cupcakes.

Ingredients:
6 ounces organic cream cheese, softened
1 cup unsalted organic butter, softened
1 tablespoon organic vanilla extract
½–1 teaspoon organic mint flavoring
6 cups organic confectioners' sugar
3–4 tablespoons organic milk
1 tablespoon Garnet Beet Puree (p. 146)

Directions:
1) Beat together the cream cheese, butter, and flavorings until light and fluffy. Slowly beat in the confectioners' sugar, adding milk as needed to make a smooth, creamy frosting.
2) Remove about ⅓ cup of the frosting and combine with about half of the beet puree to color the frosting bright pink.
3) Using a small spoon or table knife blade, carefully spread the colored frosting in a narrow stripe up one side of a large pastry bag fitted with a star tip. Add the white frosting to the bag, then swirl over each cupcake (because of the large quantity of frosting involved, you may wish to repeat this step partway through). If you're not feeling quite this adventuresome, simply frost the cupcakes and swirl a tiny dab of the pink frosting over each with a serrated knife or a fork, or add the beet puree to the frosting to color it pink.

Graham Cracker Stackers

Here's a fun way to turn Homemade Graham Crackers into dessert. As with Stuffed Apples (p. 180), there can be any number of variations. I've listed a few of my favorites here.

Ingredients:
Homemade Graham Crackers (p. 159)
Filling options:
Organic soy butter or tree nut butter and sliced bananas
Organic chocolate hazelnut spread or Chocolate Ganache (directions follow) and sliced organic strawberries or apples
Strawberry Buttercream Filling (directions follow) or Pineapple Cream Cheese Frosting (p. 197)

Directions:
1) Assembly is kid-friendly. Spread one side of each graham cracker with the desired filling, sandwiching the fruit in between. For the buttercream filling or frosting, simply spread one cracker with a bit of it and place the other graham on top.

Chocolate Ganache
Ingredients:
¼ cup organic cream
½ cup organic semi-sweet chocolate chips

Directions:
1) Heat the cream just to boiling in a small pan. Remove from the heat and stir in the chocolate chips until they are completely melted. Allow it to cool slightly; it will thicken as it cools.
2) This is best stored in a tightly covered container at room temperature and used within 2–3 days.

Strawberry Buttercream Filling
Ingredients:
¼ cup organic butter, softened
1¼ cups organic confectioners' sugar
1 tablespoon finely diced organic strawberry

Directions:
1) Cream the butter until light. Add in the confectioners' sugar and diced strawberry, beating until everything is smooth and creamy. It's better to have this frosting a little stiff, as the juices in the strawberry have a tendency to seep out the longer it sits.

Can't Be Beet Chocolate Cupcakes

The element of surprise is always fun in kids' recipes. Try a little family baking project some rainy fall day using this unexpected ingredient to make yummy chocolate cupcakes. I guarantee nobody will suspect that they contain beets unless you tell them. These are moist, chocolatey, and fine textured, delicious with either of the accompaniment choices listed below.

Makes 24 cupcakes—enough to feed a class, with maybe a few left over for the adults.

Ingredients:
24 paper baking cups and organic nonstick cooking spray or organic butter and flour
¾ cup Garnet Beet Puree (p. 146)
1⅞ cups organic sugar
½ cup organic vegetable oil
¼ cup organic unsalted butter, melted
1½ teaspoons organic vanilla extract
2 large organic eggs
2 cups unbleached organic all-purpose flour
1 teaspoon baking soda
1½ teaspoons baking powder
1 teaspoon sea salt
⅔ cup unsweetened organic cocoa powder
1 cup very hot tap water

Directions:
1) Adjust your oven rack to the upper middle position, then preheat the oven to 350° F. Place the baking cups in muffin tins then coat them lightly with nonstick spray, or generously grease and flour the tins.
2) Set aside 1 tablespoon of the puree if you plan to make Peppermint Swirl Frosting (p. 191).
3) Beat together the sugar, oil, butter, vanilla, eggs, and the rest of the beet puree.
4) In a separate bowl, combine the flour, baking soda, baking powder, sea salt, and cocoa powder. Add to the butter mixture, then mix until smooth. Add in the water, again beating until smooth.
5) Pour the batter into the prepared cupcake tins. Bake until the tops spring back when touched, about 20 minutes. Allow to cool completely before frosting them with Peppermint Swirl Frosting or Chocolate Whipped Cream (p. 196).

Chocolate Whipped Cream

This contains quite a bit less sugar than standard frosting recipes and is much loved by kids. We used it to frost our cupcakes in the spring, when fresh strawberries were available for topping them off! Unfortunately, it's not great for sending to school in advance unless you have a way to keep the cupcakes cool, either by dropping them off shortly before they're shared or checking to see if there is temporary refrigerator space available at the school. In cooler weather, a good-sized cold pack might do the trick, as long as the cupcakes are adequately covered to prevent any possible leakage. If you're making this for something other than 2 dozen cupcakes, decrease the ingredients commensurately.

Makes enough to frost 24 cupcakes.

Ingredients:
2 cups organic heavy cream
1 cup organic confectioners' sugar
1 teaspoon organic vanilla extract
¼ cup organic unsweetened cocoa powder

Directions:
1) Combine all the ingredients in a medium bowl. Beat with an electric beater until thick and creamy. Making sure the bowl and beaters are both cold will make the whipping process more efficient.
2) Use to top as desired.

> **Tip:** For times when you need a smaller amount—when topping Chocolate Pudding Cups (p. 183), for instance— it's very easy to halve or quarter the ingredients.

Pineapple Cream Cheese Frosting

This makes a lovely, creamy frosting with the light and fresh taste of pineapple. It produces more than enough for 18 cupcakes, even when decoratively swirled on. Be sure to refrigerate the frosted cupcakes if they are not going to be eaten within a few hours.

Ingredients:
¾ cup unsalted butter, softened
4 ounces organic cream cheese, softened
1 teaspoon organic vanilla extract
4 cups organic confectioners' sugar
Pinch of sea salt
3 tablespoons reserved pineapple juice (from Parsnip Cupcakes, p. 199)

Directions:
1) Beat the butter, cream cheese, and vanilla until smooth.
2) Add the confectioners' sugar and salt, then beat well.
3) Add the pineapple juice and beat on high speed until light and fluffy.
4) Swirl on the Parsnip Cupcakes and enjoy.

Tip: If you have any leftover frosting, it makes a dandy sandwich filling for Homemade Graham Crackers (p. 159).

Parsnip Cupcakes

Parsnips are one of those underrated veggies usually relegated to soups and stews. In this recipe they play a new and exciting starring role! Their mellow flavor combines nicely with the pineapple, coconut, and spice. Because parsnips are sometimes a little tricky to find, shredded carrots can be substituted in a pinch. This recipe makes 18 cupcakes. However, if you're baking for a class of 19 or 20, just divvy the batter up a little differently so you have enough to make those extra cupcakes; I won't tell if you don't.

Makes 18 cupcakes.

Ingredients:

18 paper baking cups
Organic nonstick cooking spray
8-ounce can organic crushed pineapple
　　packed in juice
3 large organic eggs
½ cup organic sugar
½ cup packed organic brown sugar
1 teaspoon organic vanilla extract
1½ cups organic all-purpose flour

1 teaspoon organic cinnamon
1 teaspoon baking soda
½ teaspoon sea salt
¼ teaspoon fresh grated organic nutmeg
¼ teaspoon organic cloves
½ cup organic vegetable oil
1½ cups shredded organic parsnips
½ cup flaked coconut

Directions:

1) Adjust your oven rack to the middle upper position, then preheat the oven to 350° F. Place the baking cups in muffin tins, then spray lightly with the cooking spray.
2) Drain the pineapple very well, reserving the juice for the frosting, then set aside.
3) Beat the eggs, sugars, and vanilla until light and fluffy.
4) Combine the flour, cinnamon, baking soda, salt, nutmeg, and cloves in a bowl.
5) In a separate bowl, combine the oil, shredded parsnips, coconut, and ½ cup crushed pineapple.
6) Add the ingredients in both bowls to the egg mixture, then beat on low speed until smooth and well blended.
7) Pour the batter evenly into the prepared tins and bake for approximately 25 minutes, until puffed, golden, and firm to touch.
8) When fully cool, frost with Pineapple Cream Cheese Frosting (p. 197).

Pie Crust Cookies

Pie Crust Cookies were a great favorite with my own kids when they were growing up. They are a simple little nibble created from the extra pie crust dough left over after rolling out for pastry shells. However, they are quite tasty enough to make all on their own!

Makes 12–16 cookies.

Ingredients:
Buttery Pie Crust dough (p. 21)
¼ cup organic milk or cream
6 tablespoons organic granulated or turbinado sugar
1 teaspoon organic cinnamon

Directions:
1) Adjust your oven rack to the upper level, then preheat the oven to 375° F.
2) If using the full batch of pie crust dough, roll half at a time into thin circles that are about 6 to 8 inches in diameter. Brush the surface of each lightly with milk or cream.
3) Combine the sugar and cinnamon. (You can also opt to simply use plain sugar without the cinnamon.) Sprinkle the surface of the rolled out dough evenly with the cinnamon-sugar mixture.
4) Using a sharp knife, cut the circle into 6 or 8 even wedges, then transfer them carefully to a parchment paper–lined baking sheet.
5) Bake for 10–15 minutes, until the cookie wedges are lightly browned around the edges. Loosen the cookies gently in case any of the sugar mixture has melted over onto the baking sheet. As with most cookies, they will be somewhat fragile until they have cooled. Once they have cooled completely, store in an airtight container until ready to send to school.

Jam Roll-ups

Here's another nice way to use some pie crust dough. These remind me of a simplified version of the traditional rugelach cookies you might see around holidays and other special occasions.

Makes 12–16 roll-ups.

Ingredients:
Buttery Pie Crust dough (p. 21), chilled
4–6 tablespoons organic fruit jam or preserves
¼ cup diced nuts, optional
¼ cup organic chocolate chips, optional (mini chips work best)

Directions:
1) Position the rack in the upper third of your oven, then preheat the oven to 375° F.
2) Divide the chilled dough into two equal portions. Form each half into a ball, roll one ball into a thin circle about 6 to 8 inches in diameter, then cut into 6 or 8 even wedges. Repeat with the second half.
3) Place a small dab of jam near the outer edge of each wedge. Sprinkle on a few nuts or chocolate chips, if you are using them. Roll each wedge, starting at the outer edge, into a crescent shape. Place on parchment paper–lined baking sheets to prevent sticking. Bake for 15–20 minutes. They should be lightly browned, but will still be slightly soft.
4) Allow to cool slightly before removing, but be sure to loosen them promptly if any preserve has leaked out so they don't stick to the baking sheet. Once they have cooled completely, store in an airtight container until ready to send to school.

Cream Cheese Sugar Cookies with Almond Icing

This is a versatile recipe that can be used for any number of special occasions. We've formed them into hearts as a special snack during our circulatory unit, and even cut them into mushroom shapes for our mycology open house. They're very tasty in other shapes as well.

Makes approximately 7 dozen cookies.

Cookie Dough
Ingredients:
1½ cups organic sugar
1 cup organic butter, softened
8 ounces organic cream cheese, softened
1 teaspoon organic vanilla extract
½ teaspoon organic almond flavoring
1 large organic egg
3½ cups organic all-purpose flour
1 teaspoon baking powder

Directions:
1) Cream together the sugar, butter, and cream cheese until fluffy. Add the vanilla, almond, and egg and beat well. Then, stir in the flour and baking powder.
2) Divide the dough in half, wrap in waxed paper or plastic wrap, and refrigerate for 1½ hours, or longer if you wish.
3) When you're ready to make the cookies, preheat the oven to 375° F.
4) Remove the dough from the refrigerator and roll it out on a floured surface to a thickness of ⅛ inch. Cut into your desired shapes with cookie cutters. Place on ungreased cookie sheets and bake for 8–10 minutes, until light golden around the edges. Carefully remove the cookies from the pans and place them onto cooling racks. Once they have cooled, enjoy them as is or decorate with a bit of Almond Icing.

Almond Icing
Ingredients:
2 cups organic confectioners' sugar
2 tablespoons organic butter, softened
¼ teaspoon organic almond extract
4–5 teaspoons organic milk

Directions:

Cream together the confectioners' sugar, butter, and flavoring. Beat in milk to make a smooth spreading consistency. This can be used either as a filling for sandwich cookies or to smooth on as icing.

Tip: If you don't want to bake 7 dozen cookies all at once, roll and cut the dough into desired shapes. Carefully place on parchment or wax paper–lined baking sheets and freeze until firm, then place in a covered freezer container with parchment paper between each layer. Label and freeze up to 1 month. Place the frozen cookies on baking sheets when you're ready to enjoy some more of them. They'll probably thaw out by the time the oven has preheated, and you'll be set to bake and enjoy your next batch!

Conversion Charts

METRIC AND IMPERIAL CONVERSIONS
(These conversions are rounded for convenience)

Ingredient	Cups/Tablespoons/Teaspoons	Ounces	Grams/Milliliters
Butter	1 cup = 16 tablespoons = 2 sticks	8 ounces	230 grams
Cheese, shredded	1 cup	4 ounces	110 grams
Cream cheese	1 tablespoon	0.5 ounce	14.5 grams
Cornstarch	1 tablespoon	0.3 ounce	8 grams
Flour, all-purpose	1 cup/1 tablespoon	4.5 ounces/0.3 ounce	125 grams/8 grams
Flour, whole wheat	1 cup	4 ounces	120 grams
Fruit, dried	1 cup	4 ounces	120 grams
Fruits or veggies, chopped	1 cup	5 to 7 ounces	145 to 200 grams
Fruits or veggies, puréed	1 cup	8.5 ounces	245 grams
Honey, maple syrup, or corn syrup	1 tablespoon	.75 ounce	20 grams
Liquids: cream, milk, water, or juice	1 cup	8 fluid ounces	240 milliliters
Oats	1 cup	5.5 ounces	150 grams
Salt	1 teaspoon	0.2 ounce	6 grams
Spices: cinnamon, cloves, ginger, or nutmeg (ground)	1 teaspoon	0.2 ounce	5 milliliters
Sugar, brown, firmly packed	1 cup	7 ounces	200 grams
Sugar, white	1 cup/1 tablespoon	7 ounces/0.5 ounce	200 grams/12.5 grams
Vanilla extract	1 teaspoon	0.2 ounce	4 grams

OVEN TEMPERATURES

Fahrenheit	Celsius	Gas Mark
225°	110°	¼
250°	120°	½
275°	140°	1
300°	150°	2
325°	160°	3
350°	180°	4
375°	190°	5
400°	200°	6
425°	220°	7
450°	230°	8

Index